How You Can Fight

Human Trafficking

OVER 50 WAYS TO JOIN THE FIGHT

Through God's Grace Ministry

Through God's Grace
P.O. Box 18065
Irvine, Ca. 92623
www.throughGodsgrace.com

Book Layout ©2013 BookDesignTemplates.com
Cover Design by "Graphic_Enamel"-Independent Graphic Artist with Elance
Graphic "Girl with Broken Chains" used in design, by DM Studio/Dreamstime

How You Can Fight Human Trafficking/ Through God's Grace. —1st ed.
ISBN 9780615973517

Contents

Disclaimer: While all attempts have been made to verify the information provided in this publication, neither the author nor the publisher assumes any responsibility for errors, omissions, etc. If you feel that information from an article you wrote was used and not referenced, please contact us and we will include the reference or send you the one we used. Please keep in mind that there are hundreds of sites with similar information on Human Trafficking. Any perceived slight of any individual or organization is purely unintentional

Internet websites offered as citation and/or sources may have changed or disappeared from the time this book was written.

Photo Disclaimer: All Photos are "Stock" photos. None of the photos are *actual* images of recruiters, victims, children viewing porn, etc.

Dedicated to the victims of Human Trafficking, law enforcement and all those organizations and individuals who are working tirelessly to protect people from being cruelly exploited by the crime of Human Trafficking.

Let my heart be broken by that which breaks the heart of God. -
Anonymous

*"There is no passion to be found playing small - in settling for a life that
is less than the one you are capable of living." -Nelson Mandela*

*"Pray as though everything depended on God. Work as though
everything depended on you." - Saint Augustine*

*"In a world where most people loath slavery, awakening their awareness
will unleash great power." - Kevin Bales*

Introduction

When I first started writing this book, the purpose was to be able to provide a resource to the ministry leaders and speakers I was training. Once it was complete, I thought "Why not make it available to whoever God may be calling to act who needed more information." If you feel that this book is a valuable resource, then do promote it through your social networking pages as God may be calling someone you know to join the fight and this book will empower them to do that.

If one wants to start a movement, one needs to create something that is very easily duplicated, which is the goal of this book. There are sections to empower leaders and simple activities that anyone can do. If you want to motivate people to act, you need to be able to communicate in a way that has them understand why their actions will make a difference. This book outlines the dynamics of human trafficking in a way that has people understand how their actions will impact this issue.

I talked to many faith communities that wanted to start a group. Some of them met, but it took a long time for them to figure out what they could do about Human Trafficking, so their group started to fall apart. I wanted to create something that would make it possible for a group to "hit the ground running." Most people are willing to volunteer 2 to 10 hours a month, so this book includes over 50 ideas that take about that much time or less. This book could easily be 300 pages or more but most people don't want to have to wade through all that. So the book is set up to be a "map" of sorts with resources under each topic. Then readers can go to the sites that address what they feel most inspired about and pursue their passion.

My mission is to inspire service groups and faith community groups to engage in several activities a year to raise awareness regarding what people can do. It might be a separate ministry or it could be a women or men's group or a subgroup of the "Social Justice" committee. For the most part, this issue is "invisible" to the average person where they live and work. We need to make it "visible."

At the website www.throughGodsgrace.com, on the Human Trafficking tab you can find handouts that you can use. (You may need to type out the entire web address in your address bar in quotes to find the site.) If you would like permission to copy sections from the book, just email me. The purpose of the book is to raise awareness and everyone is welcome to use as much as they want in their efforts to inspire people to act.

So why did I bother to copyright the book? I did that to motivate you to refer to this book as the source for anything you copy as that will increase book sales and make more people aware of what they can do. I also wanted control of who uses the information as the pimps who are trafficking kids will try to take down anyone who they feel is a threat.

If you like the book, *Please Post* a review at Amazon.com as it will help the book to sell and raise more awareness with more people. If you would like to provide an endorsement that I can include in future issues, please email that to me. If you have suggestions for how to improve the book, please do let me know. I need examples from other countries other than the U.S. as to what people are doing. There isn't room to include lists of all the organizations that are working to fight this issue. If you have an organization like that, do post what you are doing at the "Freedom Registry" or "Engage Together" so people can find you. I want the book to work for everyone and I appreciate any contributions you may have.

If you have an organization that is fighting Human Trafficking and want to do a similar book in Spanish, outlining what organizations to support in Mexico or South America etc., you are welcome to "borrow" as much as you need from this book. The same goes for a book in German, Italian, etc. Just write to me and let me know how you plan on using it at "ucanfightht@throughGodsgrace.com."

This book is the result of much prayer and conversations with well over a hundred people including the police, victims, homeland security, social workers, health professionals, teachers, community and faith leaders, conference speakers and people just like you. All the examples in this book are true. In other words, when I stated that a 12 year old girl was pimping out her friends, that example came from a woman I talked to who works with social workers. I purposely did not use the names of the people I have talked to as they are all busy people and don't want people calling them. However if you are a reporter who wants to raise awareness, you can email me and I will give you the name of the person you can interview for what you want to reference in this book. If you would like to do a book review, there is a media kit at our website on the "Human Trafficking" tab.

I clearly am not a writer, so for those of you who are accomplished writers, this book may be painful to read. Sorry. However stepping out without having it all together is one of the themes of this book. If we all waited until we were confident we were great at something before acting to make a difference, there would be very few people getting the help they need in this world.

You are welcome to post at the Facebook page "How you can fight Human Trafficking," with posts of what you are doing that are making a difference. (Just type "How You Can Fight" to find it.) As soon as you type in the words "Human Trafficking" you will get hundreds of pages you have to wade through!) People need ideas of what others are doing. I see this book as a community project, growing over time with the contribution of all those engaged in the fight.

I am a trained motivational speaker and experienced business consultant and I am available to speak on what individuals and groups can do to fight trafficking. I offer a leadership training to develop ministries for Faith communities in Southern California that are addressing Social issues. My current mission is to develop speakers and leaders so that together we can rapidly raise awareness regarding Human Trafficking and empower people to get out there and FIGHT! I pray that this book empowers you to discover your part in ending the cruel exploitation of men, women and children!

May God bless you in your efforts,

Susan Patterson for "Through God's Grace" Ministry

CHAPTER ONE

So What Does Human Trafficking Look Like?

There are those of you who are clear that you have been called to engage in the fight against Trafficking and are looking for ways to do that. Others bought this book and told yourself you are just curious as to what can be done. God has heard the cries of the victims and He is calling legions of people to join the fight. How God works is that until you choose to participate, you will find yourself thinking about the victims a lot, feeling restless distracted from your daily life. You will find no peace until you act. I know this from personal experience. So let the journeys begin!

In the book "Not in My Town" by Dillon Burroughs and Charles Powell, the most important point the authors made is that the Traffickers are not that afraid of Law Enforcement. Who they are afraid of is *You*. What that means is what worries the Traffickers and their partners the Pornographers the most, is a mobilized community. What that looks like is a community that knows what to look for and calls the police when they see something that "doesn't look right;" a community that has trained it's mail carriers how to monitor neighborhoods; a community that has run the illegal massage parlors out of town; a community that arrests recruiters who are soliciting teens at malls and school campuses, not just make them leave the mall or school. Now that is a community that will drive the Traffickers out.

How about a community whose faith communities and schools are promoting the importance of purchasing Fair Trade products at their yearly fairs and their Farmer's Markets; a community whose citizens are doing their part to reduce porn addiction by taking advantage of opportunities like their 4th of July parade to raise awareness regarding the "Opt In" campaign, a business regulation that started in England that requires all internet providers to block all porn for the entire country, unless one contacts their internet provider to "opt in" to make porn available to their household. That is a community that is doing its part to reduce the demand for both labor and sex trafficking worldwide. Is that the kind of community you want to create? Then this book is for you.

Whenever I speak, I am always asked two questions. One is "What does Human Trafficking look like in (name of city)?" The other question is "What can I as a (nurse, teen, homemaker, teacher, attorney, businessman, etc.) do about it?" This chapter answers the first question. The second chapter addresses what it will take to engage, stay motivated and end it. The remaining twelve chapters answer the question "What can I do?" Please note that for this book, not all the stories are referenced. That is intentional. Many victims and workers want to remain anonymous.

The International Labor Organization updated their statistics in May of 2014 and now report that Human Trafficking generates 150 billion in annual profits with sex trafficking generating 99 billion of that amount. (1.1) While sex trafficking takes up 2/3rds of the money, the ILO estimates that 2/3rds of the over 27 million slaves in the world are labor trafficking victims. The UN estimates that minors make up 27% of all Trafficking victims worldwide. With drugs you can only sell your product once and if you are caught with illegal drugs, a conviction is ensured. A sex trafficking victim can be sold over and over again and may be too frightened to testify against their master. Given how lucrative this crime is and the skyrocketing demand for sex and cheap goods, Human Trafficking has become the fastest growing illegal enterprise in the world.

Statistics can be confusing if you take them out of context. The U.S. Postal Inspection Service states that Identity Theft is the fastest growing crime in the U.S., but it is not under the category of "illegal enterprise." (In case you googled "fastest growing crime in the U.S.") Drugs are the largest illegal enterprise in size with Human Trafficking and Arms Trafficking almost tied for being the second largest. However given how fast Human Trafficking is growing, it is on a path to surpass drugs in size unless we take a stand and engage our communities to take action.

The National Center for Missing and Exploited Children estimate between 100,000 to 300,000 kids under the age of 18 are at risk of becoming exploited in the U.S. *(1.2)* To put this in perspective, minors made up 32% of the recued victims for the 2014 Super Bowl Sting. The Orange County, California Human Trafficking Victims Report for 2014 reported 58% adults and 42% rescued minors for that county. Contrary to popular belief, in the U.S. close to 70% of victims are U.S citizens. People in the developed countries are often surprised to find out that Trafficking is happening in their own neighborhoods. What they don't realize is that there are porn addicts in everyone's neighborhood which is creating the demand and the more affluent the area, the more money a Trafficker is going to make. "The State of Human Trafficking in California 2012" report states that a Trafficker can make well over half a million dollars per year creating an incentive to become a criminal.

In the industrialized countries like the U.S., Europe and Canada, the majority of Trafficking is sex trafficking because it is more lucrative than labor trafficking. The U.S. Department of Justice tells us that 82 percent of reported human trafficking incidents in the United States between January 2008 and June 2010 involved allegations of sex trafficking; labor trafficking accounted for 11 percent of incidents; and other or unknown forms of human trafficking made up the remaining 7 percent. In order to be considered a Trafficked victim, the victim needs to be under 18 or working as a result of fraud, coercion or force. So a prostitute who willingly entered the life at the age of 18 would not be considered a Trafficking victim. However many prostitutes entered the life before they were under 18. *(1.2)*

The reason why people ask the question...... "What does Human Trafficking look like" is because even if Human Trafficking is happening right in front of them, they don't "see" it, because they don't understand what they are looking at. The greatest weakness the Human Traffickers have is that what they do is very hard to hide if you know what to look for. That is why it is so important to educate people so they recognize what Trafficking "looks like" so they know when to call the police.

So how does Trafficking happen where you live? Porn has become a sophisticated marketing tool to create "buyer demand" for expensive acts. When one goes to porn sites, there are seductive pop-ups that one can click on that leads the user to more violent sites with younger and younger victims. After a while the porn user gets "turned on" and wants satisfaction. However they know most women would not be willing to participate in the kind of violent acts they have just seen or they need very young girls, so they go to "escort" sites to find girls/women who according to the ads "will engage their every fantasy." All the porn user has to do is "click" on a banner ad or pop-up at the porn site to find an escort site. It is clear from the pictures in the ads that many of the girls and boys are often well under 18. At the "escort" sites are drop-down menus where they can select hair color, height, bust size, etc. *(1.3)* Once they have made their selection, they can arrange a "client meet" within an hour. *(1.3)*

One of the most likely places for a "client meet" is a luxury apartment complex during the lunch hour or right after work. These apartments are located in affluent areas because that is where the most money can be made. The traffickers obtain short term leases and the women and girls are rotated through as "clients" want variety. *(1.3)* What neighbors see are business men in suits and ties and since most people who live in luxury apartments would not think that prostitution is happening in their affluent community, right next door to where they live, they rarely call the police. The bottom line is that if you see men coming and going from any home, motel or apartment, the police want you to call them.

A community that knows when to call the police is a community the

"Clients" can arrange a "meet" from an escort site in less than an hour.

Traffickers will avoid. In one case, the Traffickers were arrested when clients at a coffee shop noticed that scantily dressed women were meeting men in at the shop and walking them across the street to a business that advertised for "bankruptcy" consulting. Customers noticed that men were coming and going from the "bankruptcy" establishment at 9 o'clock at night. In some Asian communities, "coffee shop" has become code for prostitution. In Spanish speaking neighborhoods, there are "Casitas" where everyone in the neighborhood knows that, that is "where the guys go." The point here is; "If it doesn't look right, then call the police."

Sometimes the victims don't "service" clients where they live but go to a local motel or hotel to do that. If there is a house or apartment in your neighborhood where you know people are living there, but there are members of the household who never walk out the front door you should be suspicious and call the police. Sometimes you might not see people through the windows because the curtains are always closed but something about that house makes you suspicious.

In that case, stay up one night watching a movie and watch out your window. You might see the other members of the household (the victims) leaving by car late at night and coming back before dawn, because they have been out servicing "clients." In these houses where sex trafficking victims live, the bedroom door is locked from the outside, the windows are nailed shut and the victims sleep mostly during the day. In the places where labor trafficking occurs, the victims often sleep on the premises where they work, usually on thin mattresses on the floor.

Many cities are becoming pro-active by having the police incorporate into their "neighborhood watch groups," information as to what "human trafficking looks like." In addition to watching for thieves and drug dealers, "neighborhood watch groups" are watching for people who can't seem to leave their house on their own. In the U.S., Homeland Security is training postmen to watch for "what doesn't look right" in neighborhoods. (1.4) If the Traffickers thought both the neighbors and postmen were watching for them, it would make them very nervous. Every city should take on these actions. The more we can do to increase the chances of a Trafficker getting caught, the less likely criminals will consider getting involved in this crime.

The women who are put to "work," on the streets in Southern California are given a quota of $1,000 a night at $50 a "session." They work from 6 P.M. until sometimes 6 A.M., 7 days a week. Since this is when most people are sleeping, the average citizen isn't aware that Trafficking is happening in their own communities. If the "girls" finish without meeting their quota, they are burned with an iron or beaten. (1.5)

In the meantime the pimps hang out laughing and talking, sometimes having a barbecue at 2 in the morning in the parking lot of the motel. They refer to each other as "businessmen," and give each other "business" advice while they hang out. If a girl isn't being successful at "closing the sale," she will be brought over to where the pimps are hanging out and "disciplined" and humiliated.

An Orange County DA shared that one girl made $25,000 for her pimp in two weeks. She was so sore, she could barely stand up and became very sick and could not hold anything down. When she complained to her pimp, he told her to take a hot bath, eat some crackers and "get back out there." Once the Traffickers have a victim, their sense of ownership is obscene. They tattoo a bar code or their name on the necks or foreheads of their "girls" and "boys." They demand complete obedience. The women are required to call their pimp "daddy," and have to ask for permission to speak to him/her.

One victim shared that because she was hungry she used some of the money she had just earned to buy herself a hamburger at McDonalds. She got the "crap" beat out of her for not following instructions to hand over *all* of the money she had earned. *(1.5)* People ask me, "What about the hotel or motel owners who are in collusion with the Traffickers, who get "kickbacks?" There have been cases where the assets of a motel were seized as any monies made in the commission of a crime can be confiscated. *(1.6)*

The Iempathize website (www.iempathize.org) has a video posted at their site to educate people as to "what trafficking looks like" at truck stops. The posted video tells the story of a truck stop in Ohio where a 15 year old girl knocked on the door of a truck to solicit the trucker for sex. In response, the trucker called the police and simply said "This doesn't look right, these girls are too young." His call resulted in the rescue of two cousins, 14 and 15 years old, who had been kidnapped 7 months before by Human Traffickers.

Keep in mind that thousands of people had eaten at the stops the cousins were forced to "service" over the 7 month period and saw the girls going from truck to truck and given the way they were dressed, they knew what they were doing. Yet no one called the police because our perception of prostitution is not to see the girls and boys as victims. We are asleep to the fact that Human Trafficking is happening in our own communities. The FBI tells us that there are thousands of kids like these cousins who had been kidnapped or picked up as runaways, who will never be rescued because the public has an attitude of "none of my business," when they see prostitutes. The Human Traffickers are counting on that attitude while these kids live in anguish.

Whenever I share about kids being abducted, the question I am almost always asked is "what are the police doing about this?!" The answer is that the police, in partnership with Homeland Security are actively going after the Traffickers but they don't have the resources to be everywhere. Also, law enforcement would be the first to tell you we are not going to "arrest" our way out of this problem. Sex Trafficking is never going to end unless communities step up and take on protecting the most likely victims and reducing porn addiction in every country. (More on this in Chapters Six, Seven and Eight.)

Labor Trafficking includes domestic servants, sweat shops, cleaning services, pornography, construction, farming, restaurant workers, elder care facilities, factories, nail salons, forced begging, to name a few. *(1.7)* Trafficked victims could be working right in your community, in retirement homes, retail stores, in homes as nannies, etc. One of the simplest things you can do that will make a difference is to download a flyer from the Polaris project, that they have in 13 different languages, letting victims know where they can get help. You can ask your pastor if you can post the flyer in the vestibule of your place of worship where people walk in. Churches have been surprised by who comes forward.

At the Vanguard University Conference in 2012, a Salvation Army staff member shared about helping rehabilitate a girl who had been a Trafficked domestic servant/slave for years without being paid. She shared with them that the one thing she was allowed to do was to go to church every Sunday. Homeland Security will tell you that this is sometimes the case with domestic servants. Their masters may beat the victims on a regular basis, but apparently they don't want to take on the wrath of God, so they do let labor trafficking victims like domestic servants go to worship. If you were to strike up a conversation with that girl, you would have gotten a sense that she could not leave her job. However no one did talk to her. It would have made a difference if a flyer had been posted at her church.

The Polaris Project tells us that if you run across someone who may look malnourished and/or acts subdued and someone else is doing all the talking for them or is keeping their papers, you should be suspicious. One victim shared that she was rescued because a neighbor near the elder care facility where she was working 18 hours a day, 7 days a week, noticed that the workers never seemed to have a day off. The neighbor became suspicious and called the police and all the workers were rescued. *(1.8)*

In the U.S. if you see something that "does not look right," call 1-888-3737-888. You can make the call anonymously. The Polaris project will assist in advising one on what actions to take and will call the proper authorities. Polaris also has a text "Be Free" that a victim can use as often victims can't risk being overheard on the phone. Please stop reading now and put this number in your cell phone and have your friends do the same. For Canada one would go to the "Human Trafficking National Coordination Centre (HTNCC)" (613) 993-2325. For European hotlines go to the anti-trafficking site and search for "human trafficking hotlines." http://ec.europa.eu/anti-trafficking. You can scroll down to "contacts" to find NGO's that may be local that you can work with.

The Traffickers have a strategic marketing plan. They share with each other the best strategies for tricking victims, how to negotiate with "clients," how to avoid getting caught, etc. The people who are familiar with their tactics describe their methods as the "Gorilla Pimp," the "Romeo Pimp" and the "CEO Pimp." Up until recently what most parents were afraid of is the "Gorilla Pimp," meaning someone who stalks and kidnaps kids like in the movie "Taken." "Gorilla Pimp" refers to a pimp who uses force. The "Romeo" and "CEO Pimp" use trickery.

One organization shared with me the story of a beautiful girl who had come to their organization for help after being picked up by gang members. Gang coercion is an example of "Gorilla Pimping." They took the girl to the school where her brother attended and told her that they would kill her brother if she told anyone or did not cooperate. Fortunately for her, she could not handle being raped 20 times a day and did tell someone, so the police were able to intervene.

"Gorilla Pimps" are not always men. A young woman met a couple of girls in a club and then lured them out to a deserted parking lot, where she sold them to a couple of gang members. Women are often used by the gangs and pimps to recruit and abduct because we don't expect a woman to be involved with Human Trafficking. *(1.9)*

The Traffickers know that you have told your children not to trust strangers so they have recruited good looking 19, 22, etc. year old guys to become "boyfriends" of girls because teens will trust someone close to their age. "The State of Human Trafficking in California 2012" report, tell us that these "boyfriends" and Traffickers of all ages will use online gaming sites, modeling sites, dating services and social media to find their victims. They hang out where teens hang out, like malls and schools. These pimps are referred to as "Romeo pimps" and they are taught every romantic trick like flattery, acting sympathetic and understanding of how difficult the teen's life is with all the restrictions their parents put on them, etc. They often buy the teen gifts. They might tell them that "they are so in love with them that they think of them every minute of every day," so the teens or women fall madly in love. If your child is showing up with lots of "gifts," you need to start asking some tough questions! A teen who is in love with a guy that their parents won't approve of will most likely keep that a secret, but she will tell her best friend which is why we need to raise awareness among all teens.

When I spoke at a church in a wealthy community, a woman came up to me at the table and shared with me that she would not have believed that what I had talked about could happen in her community, except that her friend's 15 year old daughter had run away to be with one of these guys. The only reason the police had been able to find the teen at the bus station where she was about to cross the state line, is because she had used her mother's credit card to buy the ticket. If her mother had not insisted that the police act right away and if the police had not found her, it would have been doubtful that, that teen would have been seen again.

At another church, a staff member shared with me that after providing training on internet safety at their church, a mother who was monitoring her daughter's computer found out that a guy 1,000 miles away had sent her 15 year old daughter a plane ticket! The training the church provided, most likely saved that girl's life.

Some parents think that if they live in a gated community, go to church every Sunday and their children go to "good" schools, they are

"Romeo Pimps" and other recruiters are at places where teens hang out, looking for potential victims.

immune to being affected by Trafficking. As a result they don't provide enough education for their children regarding this problem, which makes their children vulnerable. For that reason, the traffickers often target girls from "good" families because they are so naive.

I heard the testimony of a girl from an affluent, "good" family who did run away with her "Romeo Pimp" when she was a teen. She shared how naïve she was. He told her that she needed to have sex with strangers because they needed to eat and she believed him. He kept moving her every few days to different hotels. She never saw any of the money they made and had no idea how much money he was making and how he was finding clients. She had been completely brainwashed into thinking her "boyfriend" loved her and they were just desperate for money which is why she had to have sex with strangers. This is a common scenario for women and girls who are exploited by the "Romeo Pimp." It took months of therapy before she started understanding the reality of what she had been involved in.

The "CEO Pimp" may use "job offers" to trick teens. In a upper middle class community the Traffickers had posted handbills at local schools, recruiting for "Summer Jobs." One father shared with me that his daughter got a text for a "modeling job." When she asked for more information regarding the "modeling opportunity," the recruiter let her know that she could make more money if she wore a bathing suit! Most likely this was what they refer to in sales as "the qualifying process." There are bathing suits that leave little to the imagination and it is a short step to complete nudity, once you get a girl to agree to have her picture taken almost nude. While this may have been a scam to find girls for pornography, pornography often leads to becoming a victim of Trafficking.

Well dressed women are approaching young girls in malls, offering them modeling jobs. Think about it. If you were a con artist who wanted to trick someone, wouldn't you show up well dressed with a clipboard, job applications and business cards? If they walked up to you at your local mall, you would probably think these are representatives of companies with legitimate job offers, because we don't expect criminals to be approaching us at public places where we feel safe. The Traffickers are counting on that perception and one "applicant" that I know of, was abducted when she went for the "job" interview.

If nothing else, a filled out job application makes identity theft possible. What makes this confusing is that there are legitimate agencies that are soliciting women for their modeling portfolio business or may be actually looking for models and they could be doing that at malls. Unfortunately, for both the massage and modeling business, these criminals are making people wary of these types of businesses. Professional modeling agencies have thousands of applicants every year. Do you really think they need to be in so many malls recruiting young girls for modeling jobs?! If your daughter wants to be a model then let her know you will call an established agency and set up an appointment for an interview.

A 12 year old from Illinois whose dream it was to be a supermodel, met a "talent scout" in a chat room she had found when looking for modeling sites. She was so excited because the con artist/agent truly understood her dream and had made many 12 year olds into supermodels. He sent her magazine covers claiming he was the agent who had made the models on the covers successful. (12 year olds will believe anything if it is what they want to hear!) The predator then told her she needed to come to Hollywood for an audition and because he *believed* in her, he sent her the plane ticket and sent a taxi to her home to pick her up. *(1.10)*

Of course, they agreed she couldn't tell her parents because her parents didn't believe a 12 year old could be a famous model and might not let her go. Fortunately for the 12 year old she got in a conversation with the flight attendant on the plane and shared with her about going to meet her "talent agent" in Los Angeles alone, without her parents. The flight attendant didn't think that "sounded right" so she told the captain who called the police. The "talent agent" was arrested at the airport and the police used his phone to find out where he lived. When they busted into his house, they found 17 young kids, 4 boys and 13 girls who were victims of Human Trafficking. They were in really bad shape, drug addicted, malnourished, desperate and fearful. *(1.10)*

The point of this story is that the parents of the 12 year old thought nothing of their 12 year old going to modeling sites and chat rooms, had no idea she had left during the night and did not know that predators target pre-teens because they are easy to manipulate. When the police do presentations for parents, they are sometimes told by naive parents that their daughter gets good grades in school and is too smart to fall for a Trafficker's tricks. They don't understand that these guys are pros. They know how to appeal to the dreams of a teenager and are not to be underestimated.

The clients tell the Traffickers what they want and sometimes they tell the pimp they want an intelligent college girl. So the CEO pimp will go into the clubs surrounding college campuses to find them. Rachel shares of having been in one of these clubs and the pimp came up to her and told her how beautiful she was. She blew him off because she knew better than to trust men who offer women modeling jobs. Then one of his models came up to her and told Rachel how glamorous her lifestyle was and how much money she was making as a model and that she should really come talk to her "agent." The "agent" invited Rachel to just "try him out" so Rachel agreed and was immediately set up with a photo shoot, then a music video shoot. (Both shoots could have been faked.) After the shoot, he told her that he needed a W-2 from her in order to pay her so she filled it out with her parent's address as her permanent address and her current address at college. If he had asked for her address, Rachel would have known better than to give it to him and the Traffickers know this so they have all kinds of tricks to get what they want.

At one point, Rachel became suspicious of the "agent's" intentions so she called him and told him, "thanks for everything, but she needed to focus on school and would not be available for any more modeling." He got very quiet and then read off her parent's address, her current address where she lived with her roommate and told Rachel he would kill all of them if she did not do everything he told her. Then he said, "Don't make me hurt you!" From there Rachel entered a life of prostitution and became one of the girls who approached other college girls in clubs to tell them to come talk to her "agent." Fortunately one of the pimp's victims finally had the courage to seek help from the police. Two years later, Rachel's pimp was sentenced to 15 years in prison. Upon his arrest, the FBI found out that this man had victimized 75+ girls for 7+ years, preying on naive college girls away from home.

Rachel's pimp was different from the Romeo Pimps and Gorilla Pimps people often hear about. To help spread awareness about this little-known type of pimping, Rachel and her husband started a company called Sowers Education Group to educate young women on how Traffickers trick women and coined the term "CEO Pimp." The second key focus of Sowers Education Group is Media Awareness: challenging students to think critically about pop culture's glorification of casual sex and pimping. *(1.8)*

The police will tell you that we really need to educate our children and women on the tactics of these pimps and their "recruiters" and to be alert to our environment. It made the difference for one woman. Upon arriving at an airport well after midnight, the woman sought an available taxi to be taken to a hotel. Since she was not familiar with the town, she didn't know what direction the taxi was supposed to go. Upon her arrival she realized she was at the wrong hotel and became suspicious. After a loud altercation with the taxi driver there was no resolution. The hotel staff heard the yelling outside and came to the woman's rescue and questioned the taxi driver. The woman's bags were taken out of the car and the taxi drove swiftly away. The woman knew to use her voice and that resulted in her rescue. The next morning she learned the taxi company was associated with a ring of Traffickers in that town.

While our focus tends to be on our pre-teen and teen daughters, the "Enough" "Internet Safety 101 Course" gives one an insight on how predators make friends with young boys and girls. Kids are getting pop-ups while they play with their online games or even at kid's sites like Nickelodeon.com. These "pop-ups" take them to predator sites. The predators talk to a kid while playing online games using software to disguise their voice so they sound like a young kid or a teenager. Predators know you have told your children not to trust strangers, but to a kid someone their age is not what you are talking about. They are thinking you mean "big, scary man." A pedophile is not considered a Trafficker unless they trade or sell the kids they have abducted, which they often do because all sex addicts are looking for variety. We have told our children not to give their address out to strangers, but all a predator has to do is convince a young kid to "friend" them through their social media. Once they have access to a kid's site, they can pull up the child's pictures and use geo-tagging to find out exactly where that child lives.

Anyone can go to You-Tube and view a video that shows one how to use geo-tagging to find out where a picture was taken. For that reason, it is important to make the GPS setting on your smart phone inactive before you take a picture that you are going to upload to any social media site or send. Once the picture is sent, the recipient can send to others and you no longer have any control of who may have your picture. With "Snap Chat," because the picture disappears after a few seconds, it leaves the user (mostly teens) with the impression that their picture "disappeared." No, it is out there on the internet for anyone to access!

At one presentation that I was leading, a man turned to his young wife and said "That's it, we aren't having daughters!" He was kidding.

We often assume only girls are at risk, but one night at around 9 P.M. my friend's 17 year old son, who is a slim 5ft. 8 inches, was skateboarding home through a nearby, pristine neighborhood of $700,000 homes (middle class community) in Orange County, California. When he stopped to tie his shoe, a man in a car stopped and said "Your mom sent me to pick you up and get you home." No, no one had sent anyone to pick up the teen. If he had gotten in the car, it is doubtful anyone would have seen him again. Most of us would not think that Traffickers or porn addicts are looking to abduct kids, especially teen boys over 16.

One of the tactics the Traffickers use to lower a kid's guard to make them easier to exploit for pornography or sex trafficking is to send teen girls porn that they can access on their cell phones. Teen boys are also receiving porn on their cells which is creating future clients for Traffickers and our future pedophiles who could be your son, your nephew, your cousin, your grandchild. The pictures boys are getting are not only from porn sites. Their female classmates are sending teen boys breast and crotch shots, which is compounding the problem. The sexualization of our society is making young people numb to this problem so the shock value is lost. As a result, teen boys think nothing of spending hours at porn sites or "pimping out" their girlfriends. They have been known to tell their girlfriend to go have sex with a guy for $50 so they can go to lunch. *(1.11)*

Social Workers are seeing girls as young as 12, solicited to become a "recruiter" for a Trafficker sometimes recruiting their friends as young as 10. These teen girl "recruiters" convince their friends to have sex for money by showing them their new cell phone or fancy clothes, etc. and boast about how much money they are making. They show them porn which desensitizes them to the damage they are doing to their spirit and emotional and physical well-being. *(1.12)* This is another example where the teen could start showing up with expensive items. You need to do an itemization of how much their allowance, etc. is and what the items they are purchasing cost. If it doesn't "seem right" it probably isn't. One father and mother started reading their daughter's diary when they got suspicious. They were horrified by what their daughter had gotten into but at least they were able to intervene and it made a difference.

The most likely victim of a Human Trafficker is a homeless kid. The National Runaway Switchboard estimates that 1.6 to 2.8 million teenagers will run away every year in the U.S. and that within 48 hours of hitting the streets, one in three will be involved in prostitution. *(1.13)* The runaways themselves will tell you that within 10 minutes of hitting the bus stations, the Human Traffickers have approached them with statements like…"Hi ya, baby. Hungry baby?"

Many of these kids will return home. However, the National Alliance to end homelessness estimates that 1/3 will wind up involved in "survival sex," either as victims of a Human Trafficker or on their own. For the homeless kids who age out of the foster care system who have no family support or are runaways from the foster care system or from abuse at home, they will become prey for all those who exploit kids.

Once these kids are picked up the Traffickers don't want the kids fighting back when they are raped by the "clients." The FBI tells us that the initial phase consists of being locked in a room for weeks and being gang raped over and over again, until they have conditioned that kid to being raped. These kids are threatened, cut, set on fire, beat and tortured. The mental, physical and emotional torture is horrific and it is being done to kids!

One teen described her experience this way: "I can't describe to you the feeling of terror. No child should ever have to know that kind of fear. I didn't know what I was going to have to endure that night, for how long, or if I was going to come back home." *(1.14)* If you ever have a chance to hear a victim's testimony, they will share that they were not afraid of death, most wanted to die but there are things worse than death that they were threatened with, like torture. Often they are threatened with the death of a family member if they do not cooperate. Sex trafficking victims are dead in less than 7 years. They will die from Aids, drug overdose, being beaten to death, etc. Many will commit suicide. Only 1% will ever be rescued. *(1.15)*

The police have a difficult job. The Traffickers/Pimps threaten the "girls" if they testify and they make good on their promise in public ways

At websites like "You Tube" one can access videos like "Pimping 101."

to keep their "girls" in line. I met a policeman who processed the evidence for Trafficked victims, meaning he knew how the pimps had terrorized and tortured the girls. During the interviews he conducted with the pimps, they were so arrogant it was all the policeman could do not to "deck" them so the policemen got himself transferred to another unit before he might do something that could possibly ruin his career. We need to pray for our law enforcement. We need to also pray for those who work with victims. The counselors I have met who work with former victims will tell you that working with Trafficking victims is the most difficult rehabilitation job there is.

In addition to the obvious abuse of treating people like slaves, what many people are unaware of is that the Traffickers have found an additional source of income, which is selling babies. At the Homeland Security website, www.ice.gov, when you search for Human Trafficking, you can find pictures and videos. One is a clip from the Lifetime movie "Baby sellers" which gives you a sense of how babies are trafficked for adoption. While most people are aware of illegal adoption scams, there are other demands for babies and little kids like child pornography, selling kids to pedophiles, etc. 19% of convicted pedophiles are found to have "baby porn." (National Center for Missing and Exploited Children) 58% of all child abuse domains are housed in the U.S. (Internet Watch Foundation) (Stats are from www.enough.org)

If one does certain searches (like young nude) on Social Media web sites, one can find pictures of little kids with their "handler" boasting about their sexual prowess in an effort to sell them. Mainly these kids are sold in the "dark' web. Drop In Centers for Prostitutes are seeing more and more pregnant prostitutes. It is heartbreaking to hear the testimony of Trafficking victims who have had their babies taken from them and to this day, they have no idea what happened to that child.

One can go to You-Tube or an online bookstore and search and get a step by step video or book on "How to be a Pimp." If you want to get an idea of what I am referring to, you can watch the video at You- Tube by Harmony Dust, a woman who now has a ministry as part of the effort to fight Trafficking. Her video is one you could show at a presentation at a church. The rest are very crude in the way they talk about women and they promote how rich one can become through Pimping.

As a result of all these "hot tips" you can get online, we have more and more teens becoming criminals. The glamorization of pimping is brainwashing kids into thinking of sex trafficking as a "business" where one can get rich, rather than thinking of it as a crime. The immaturity of teens is making them prime targets to be "sold" on the idea of becoming a recruiter which is why we have 12 year olds pimping out their friends. Interestingly enough the books and videos don't mention the part of how high the incidence of Aids is among sex trafficking victims and the fact that there is so much public outrage over Trafficking that when we lock Traffickers up, we pretty much throw away the key!

The problem in Europe is growing with organized crime in the Balkans providing victims to their counterparts throughout Europe. The women and young boys are lured with promises of jobs and education opportunities. 60% of Trafficking victims in Europe are European citizens. (1.16) The victims think they are going to destination countries like the UK for a better life so they are happy and excited about their future.

This makes it very difficult for the police to identify them at checkpoints, because they don't look like trafficking victims. Often, it is only when they arrive and are forced into a life of degradation do they realize they have been tricked.

Prostitution is legal in Canada which made it a destination country for girls from the Ukraine and all over the world. Organized crime would promise these girls jobs and then take their passports when they got off the plane. Canada made a move to fight trafficking by banning foreign strippers, escorts and massage-parlor workers. All countries where prostitution is legal should consider passing a law like this as it has reduced foreign sex trafficking in Canada. However, now those involved in the commercial sex industry in Canada are advertising these jobs to High School kids as a way to pay for their college education. *(1.17)*

Australia is a destination country for women being brought in from Asia. "Project Respect," one of the main groups in this country fighting trafficking, feels that one of the reasons for this demand is racialized ideas that Asian women are more compliant and will accept higher levels of violence, which is in demand given how violent porn has become. This information comes from www.HumanTrafficking.org which provides an overview for what Human Trafficking "looks like" for 18 different countries. It is an outstanding website.

Cell phones are more available to people in Third World countries than drinking water. *(1.18)* As often happens with this crime, the Traffickers are using technology to trick poor women. Women are receiving ads for jobs, a better life on their cell phones. *(1.19)* Sometimes these ads take the form of recruitment for "child brides," which is considered another form of Trafficking. Thankfully, there is a growing movement of women educating other girls in the Third World that these ads are lies.

Child Soldiers is another form of Trafficking. Amnesty International tells us that hundreds of thousands of children are recruited as soldiers worldwide. While mostly boys are kidnapped or recruited, girls are kidnapped to cook and clean for the soldiers and act as in-house prostitutes. The danger and brainwashing these children are exposed to is horrific. If this form of trafficking touches your heart, there are many organizations to support that are working to save children from becoming child soldiers. You can raise awareness for these children by showing the inspiring movie "Machine Gun Preacher" which is on Netflix.

Organ trafficking is a growing problem in countries like South America, Africa India and China. Children are kidnapped as the cornea in a baby's eye is @70% of the size of an adult cornea. The documentary "Hot, Human Organ Trafficking" on Netflix is a good movie to watch if you want to know more about this type of trafficking.

The complete lack of respect for the life and dignity of another human being is a theme that one finds with regard to all types of trafficking throughout the world. This book focuses on what the individual and groups can do to end Trafficking in industrialized countries like the U.S. If you are looking for a world view of this problem, Kevin Bales Pulitzer nominated book "Ending Slavery" provides an insight into the worldwide dynamics of Trafficking, government efforts, the politics that affect this issue and the cultural shift that needs to happen to end Trafficking. The "TIP" report is also a great reference. Just Google "Trafficking in Persons 2013/2014 report," or go to the U.S. Department of State site.

A truly eye opening movie entitled "Tricked" is on Netflix. There is something about hearing testimonies of both the pimps and the victims that makes this issue very real. However for some this movie overwhelms them and drives them into resignation because the movie is brutal. They feel that the problem is so big, they personally won't be able to make a difference. (See Chapter Two on motivating people to act.) What may inspire you and move you into action is the movie "Amazing Grace." It is the true story of one man's stand to end slavery in England. It is a great movie to show at a place of worship.

In Thailand, the children are gathered behind a gate. As dark begins to fall, the men gather around smoking. Then the gate opens and for $5 you get a session with a child where you can do whatever you want. For $30 you can have that child for a night. Upon witnessing this, one woman on a mission trip fell to the ground weeping in anguish, crying out to God to save His children. (1.20) After listening to all these stories, are you ready to say "ENOUGH?!" Then keep reading.

References: *(1.1)* *Statistics* *are* *at* *this* *web* *link.* http://www.ilo.org/global/topics/forced-labour/lang--en/index.htm

(1.2) Child Prostitution, The Commercial Sexual Exploitation of Children, online site for gvnet.com/child prostitution/USA.htm taken from article: "U.S. sex trade consumes thousands of children." Jeff Johnson, One News Now, 7/22/2008.

(1.3) Conversation with Orange County, California Vice Cop and DA.

(1.4) From the U.S. Homeland Security website.

(1.5) Presentation by Pastor Paula Daniels of Forgotten Children.

(1.6) Conversation with an officer from the OC, Human Trafficking Task Force.

(1.7) From the Polaris website

(1.8) Field Conference by Congressman Royce, 10/13/13

(1.9) Presentation by Sowers Education.

(1.10) Presentation by L.A. County Prosecutor, Cyber Exploitation Conference, Sister of St. Joseph, OC center, 10/19/2013

(1.11) Conversation with Homeland Security.

(1.12) Conversation with a Crittenton staff member

(1.13, 1.14) Child Prostitution, The Commercial Sexual Exploitation of Children, online site for gvnet.com/child prostitution/USA.htm taken from article: (1.13) Horror of teen sex slavery not foreign woe; it's here. Alan Johnson, The Columbus Dispatch, January 25, 2009. (1.14) (Teen Prostitution in America. David Rosen, Counter Punch, August 2 / 3, 2008 and article: Former US Teenage Prostitutes Escape Brutal Street Life Mike O'Sullivan, Voice of America VOA News, Los Angeles, June 18, 2009

(1.15) Stat posted at The A21 Campaign site.

(1.16) The Star.com, World. 11.26.13. In EU, Most Human Trafficking Victims are European, Experts Say.

(1.17) Huffington Post, Canada – The Blog, 7/27/2012. Joy Smith, MP, (member of parliament) "Are Sex Traders Targeting Your Teenage Daughter?"

(1.18) The book "Twitter for Good, by Claire Diaz-Ortiz.

(1.19) Joanna Butrin, 2014 Human Trafficking conference, Vanguard University.

(1.20) Human Trafficking Conference, Saddleback Church, 01.11.14

CHAPTER TWO

What Will It Take to End It

Most business models consist of supply, demand and the middle man/woman. If you destroy any one of the three components to the business model, the business collapses. With Human Trafficking, law enforcement can take care of the "middle man" or the Trafficker, but the efforts of law enforcement alone is not enough to end Trafficking. We need the entire community to engage in the fight to address the "demand" and "supply" side of trafficking. Many of the victims that make up the "supply" side of sex trafficking in the U.S. are kids, mainly street kids. The demand side for sex trafficking is being driven by pornography addiction. The demand for labor trafficking in the Third World is being created by people in the industrialized countries unwittingly purchasing products made by slaves.

We need to organize ourselves to motivate millions to take sufficient, effective action that includes both a top down and bottom up approach to address the supply, demand and middle man/woman aspects of Trafficking. For example "top down" law enforcement can strengthen laws, while citizen groups can put out flyers to raise awareness so that victims know where they can get help. The police really need our partnership to raise awareness regarding "what trafficking looks like" so people know when to call the police. This chapter refers to the cultural shift that needs to occur to engage enough people to join the fight so that Trafficking can end. Parts may be difficult to grasp, but if you can become facile with the distinctions in this chapter, you will be a powerful leader in the fight. All the succeeding chapters after this one, address specific actions one can take.

While you read this book, start thinking about who you would want to work with. It may be your prayer group, your friends, your women's or men's group, your service club, etc. We can do so much more when we partner with others and we tend to lose motivation when we act alone. Also keep in mind that we need to open ourselves to God in all that we do. In his book, "Radical," David Platt expresses it this way "Yes, we work, we plan, we organize and we create, but we do it all while we fast, while we pray and while we confess our need for the provision of God."

In his book, "Crossing the Threshold of Hope," John Paul the II made two critical points. The first was that over 2/3rds of the people in the world share the same values as part of their Faith Walk, including helping the poor, protecting the innocent, etc. The other point he made is that we have the resources to end every social justice issue that exists. Research validates that statement. For instance, Josette Sheeran, Executive Director of the UN World Food Programme tells us we can end hunger in our generation. *(2.1)* Hunger/poverty is one of the barriers to world peace and is one of the root causes of many issues like Human Trafficking as very poor mothers will become prostitutes in order to feed their children. One of the main points of the Pope's book is that while we have the resources, what is missing is the "will" to end issues like hunger and Trafficking.

So why is the 'will" to end hunger, trafficking, etc. missing? I have heard various responses to that question from "people don't care" to "someone needs to do something about this" and that "someone" is almost always flawed in some way. The "someone" is often the government, law enforcement, etc. Behavioral scientists tell us that people do not respond to the "facts" of an issue or problem. They respond to their "perception" of the facts. *(2.2)* In other words the person who perceives mountain climbing to be fun and challenging is going to be more likely to climb the mountain than one who perceives it as dangerous and hard work. If you want to create the "will" to fight, if you want to motivate people to act you need to become facile with three aspects of human behavior. They are "perception," "bringing it home" and "common ground."

Perception: The pimps refer to themselves as businessmen and their victims as "business women" who are using the gift that God gave them. Doesn't sound like they are bad people, now does it?! (Sarcastic statement.) Many smokers will tell you that smoking helps them relax because of the ads they see with people relaxing with a cigarette. The fact is that smoking is a stimulant. Both of these examples illustrate that people act based on their perception, even if that perception isn't true. Perception is that powerful. The whole business of advertising is to create perceptions that "sell" the product. We need to create perceptions that motivate people to act to fight Trafficking. So how do we do that?

Why people lack the "will" to take action is not because they are selfish, etc. It is because social issues are portrayed as overwhelming with stats in the thousands or hundreds of millions, without telling people what they can personally do about the issue. Behavioral scientists tell us that making problems appear larger than one's ability to resolve the problem will drive people into resignation and often paralyze them. As a trained motivational speaker, I know from experience that people want to make a difference but they will be reluctant to act if they don't think they can win. They won't act if they don't know what to do. When you provide working models of what other people are doing and show your audience the difference that project is making, people will take on that project.

For example, when I do trainings and encourage groups to put up flyers, I let them know that when victims are rescued and asked why they didn't try to escape, the victims tell their rescuers they didn't know where they could get help. When I let them know that trafficking victims have been rescued after seeing a poster at a health clinic or a church, they now understand why that action will make a difference. They immediately begin a conversation as to who they know or what group they should ask to help them put out flyers.

I also let the group know that of the five most populated countries in the world, the U.S. ranks as number three. The Polaris Project has charts that show that of the top five, which include China, India, Indonesia and Brazil, the U.S. is in the category of "Trafficking is Illegal, but Problems Exist." The other four countries are designated as "Trafficking is Limitedly Illegal and is Practiced." What this means is that the U.S., given its population, could be the main purchaser of products produced by Slaves. Kevin Bales' book "Ending Slavery" illustrates that from the carpets we walk on, the shoes on our feet, the sugar, coffee, tea and seafood we eat, to the electronics we buy, could have been made by slaves.

Given what a huge impact the U.S can make on reducing child and slave labor, the audience then pays rapt attention as I outline simple things they can do like having a table at their annual church fair to raise awareness and other actions like selling "Fair Trade" chocolate at Easter. (More on this in Chapter Five) The average person wants to know what they can do in 2 to 10 hours a month that with very little effort will make a big difference. If you are successful at convincing people of that, they will act.

Convincing people to act doesn't mean telling them that the project will be easy, when in fact it will be difficult. It is about putting things into perspective and challenging people. People respond in a positive way to being challenged and where they have the opportunity to be a hero or heroine. When I took on becoming a foster mom at the age of 51 to a 6 year old, my social worker told me it would be hard, but not hard 24/7. That statement both prepared me and made it possible for me to consider doing something I had been very much afraid of doing.

The inspiring book "Tattoos of the Heart," by Father Gregory Boyle, clearly outlines how brutal life can be in gang communities but leaves one with the sense that through community partnerships and compassion, even gang communities can be turned around. Martin Luther King Jr., is an example of an effective leader who broke down the problem so that people could recognize where they could play their part, which is the purpose of this book. Both Father Boyle and Martin Luther

King Jr. created a perception of the problem in a way that gave people the sense that they could win and that their actions would make a difference, so they joined them in their fight.

Given how much influence the media has, they have the power to change the world with regard to Human Trafficking and many social issues. In order to do that, they need to take note of studies that document what drives behavior. I am referring to presenting stories in a way that motivates people to want to get out there and FIGHT! Presenting stories with a lot of drama which overwhelms people with how terrible the incident is with no real solution drives people into resignation and fear, the feeling of "I can't do anything about it so my focus needs to be on protecting my own needs and family."

A better approach that would create positive change would be to tell a story, say perhaps of a husband killing his wife and then present stories of what people in the community are doing to fight domestic violence. Then people would be left with the experience that while the incident is tragic, they live in a caring world made up of heroes and heroines. Then they would be inspired to act if they live in that community or would

The media can inspire others to join the fight.

start thinking along the lines of what they could do with regard to the social problems they are concerned about. The media may feel that they are already doing this, but I speak in front of over 20,000 people a year and what I have found is that people don't know what action they can personally take on almost any social issues unless they are actively engaged in the issue by volunteering for an organization that is helping a population like the homeless or victims of domestic violence, etc.

Instead of coming to work sharing stories in the lunch room of the latest terrible story they heard, which only leaves people lamenting how terrible it all is, they could share the news story and the way people are making a difference. People tend to share what they are inspired about and there may be someone in that lunch room that needs the services of that organization or wants to volunteer for that organization. The point is that the way stories are often presented; there is a missed opportunity to create awareness of what people can do to change lives. Often the media does try to inspire us with stories of heroes and heroines, but sometimes showing the kind of people in CNN's "Heroes" or the book "Half the Sky" can be like reading about the Saints, that while inspiring it can also drive us into complacency because we know we can never attain that level of heroism.

You need a mix of stories of people like Mother Theresa and stories of the local guy on the street who took a small action that made a difference, so people can identify with someone like themselves. David Batson did a beautiful job of this in his book "Not for Sale," which illustrated the difference made by everyday people taking action with what was right in front of them. While this is being done more and more often in news programs and websites like MSN, etc. what is missing is the sense that we can win or are winning.

Unless you convince people that they can win, many won't bother to act. Telling a story here and there of what some individual did does not necessarily leave people with a picture in their head that we are making progress that the goal is in sight. In order to convince people that we can win, you need to let them know that we have the resources to win and show them how they can participate. I accomplish this when I speak at churches by letting people know that there are ten churches in California for every child that needs to be adopted in that state, but only 25% of kids who are adoptable ever get adopted. *(2.3)* For those who "age out" of the foster care system, almost half will become homeless and could very likely become victims of Human Trafficking. Then I outline the actions the group can take to promote adoption so kids don't hit the streets. This approach motivates them to act because that statistic creates the perception that we have the resources to win. People will act if they feel bigger than the problem and go into avoidance if they don't feel that they have the ability to make a difference.

For the most part the media reports on incidents but rarely uses the approach that we have the resources to win, that we can overcome any social problem, most likely because the reporters themselves are not convinced that that is true. When I asked reporters why they don't provide resources for people to act when they report on an issue like "gang violence," the response is often that, that is not a part of their job. While many reporters do consider that part of their job is to share what actions people can take that will make a difference and do include that as part of their programs, we need to ask *all* reporters to make that a part of their job. Many reporters choose that career because they want to make a difference and one way to do that is to be more socially responsible for how they report the news.

One of the points Eddie Bynum made in his book "Justice Awakening," is that although CNN is a "breaking news" network, they decided to use their global resources and influence to expose Human Trafficking and unite people around the world in the fight with their "CNN Freedom Project." I can't say enough for what an outstanding job they did to give voice to the victims, to bring captors to justice and to inspire everyone with their stories of unprecedented courage from every day people who are fighting back. As more and more radio, TV and print media are going beyond just "breaking news" to inspiring people to join the fight the movement toward ending slavery will be accelerated.

Community leaders, individuals and reporters have a social responsibility to do enough research so that people are clear that we have enough resources to create a world that works for everyone and speak in a way that convinces people of that. Then people will act to create needed change. Any story that demonstrates the Triumph of the Human Spirit over social injustice like CNN did with their "Freedom Project," inspires us which is why it is important to be around others who speak for what is possible and avoid those who unwittingly seek to bury us in resignation.

By giving the public the sense that we are getting organized, that thousands are joining the fight, more will join. We saw this kind of phenomenon with the Tunisian Facebook Revolution. *(2.5)* Once we reach a critical mass of awareness with enough people involved in the fight, the incidence of Human Trafficking will begin to decline. An example of creating this type of public perception is the creation of "New York New Abolitionists," (www.nynewabolutionists.com) and the NYC Price of Life Campaign (October 2013) which united over 75+ organizations with events all over the city, including 15 college campuses and 60 traveling art stations engaging people in the streets on the issue of trafficking. http://priceoflifenyc.org. That event engaged the entire community and accelerated the movement in New York City to fight Trafficking.

As one reads through biography after biography of the Abolitionists who are fighting Human Trafficking in New York city and the groups who are engaged in the fight, one is left with the sense that God has called an army to fight for kids and that there is enough power there to win. That sense inspires others to want to join the fight. If this display of solidarity were to be done in every city, the incidence of Trafficking would decline. It would alter the perception of the Traffickers and their clients from feeling that they are "hiding in plain sight," to the sense that they can no longer hide, that they will be caught.

Perception is created by how one *describes* the situation or problem. A great leader *describes* a future that doesn't exist yet and convinces people that future is not only possible, but can and will happen if they join him/her. (2.4) If they are successful at convincing people to take action, then the new future will happen and everyone will talk about that leader as a great visionary. Yes, leaders like Martin Luther King had vision but it was their ability to enroll enough people to take action that made the new future possible.

The fact is that we do have the resources to win. The only reason the Traffickers are winning is because they are organized and we are not. There are far more "good" guys than there are "bad" guys. If the "good" guys established world wide networks that were stronger than the world wide networks the Traffickers have, we would win. The fastest way to establish those networks is by empowering nationwide organizations like churches or service clubs to do activities and set up ministries.

Bringing it Home: The second major aspect of human behavior that a leader needs to be facile with that creates the "will" to fight any great injustice is to make it personal, to "bring it home." In other words, as long as we perceive Human Trafficking to be a problem in another country with another group of people other than ourselves, another part of the city, etc. our motivation to fight will be low. I heard the testimony of a tough FBI agent who had participated in rescuing kids and processing the evidence. At one point, when he was describing what the kids had been forced to endure he choked up as he began this sentence...

We need to protect our children from becoming cruelly exploited.

"If this had happened to my daughter..." He had to stop for a few seconds to pull himself together and then finished his presentation. That man had brought Human Trafficking "home" to himself which inspired his commitment to fight.

Whenever I speak, I provide examples of "what Human Trafficking looks like" and then ask people in the audience if their teens have been solicited at malls, if they know where prostitution is happening in their community, etc. When audience participants bring up local malls or massage parlors where someone was solicited that is only a few blocks away, throughout the room are heard spontaneous comments like "OMG, I shop there." Or my daughter goes to that mall!" Or I had no idea this was happening right where I live!" Once people have shared local examples, I then have the rapt attention of the audience for what they need to do.

One of the best ways to bring Human Trafficking "home" with your group is to participate in a "street outreach" project to homeless teens or do an activity together with foster kids. Interacting with a kid who is vulnerable to becoming trafficked will motivate anyone to act to protect them. Another way is to share victim's stories who have been trafficked in your own community. You can find these stories from the police social workers and those who work with victims.

If you truly believed that if you did not act, your daughter, son, grandchild, etc. was going to become the next victim of Human Trafficking, I could stop here. You would figure out what to do and you would not stop until there wasn't one Trafficker left on the planet! The fact is that for the Traffickers this is big business. They can make anywhere from $80,000 to $500,000 off of each victim per year. (2.6) The younger the victim, the more money that can be made. That much money is a tremendous incentive to find kids to sell, which is why the Traffickers ARE in your world. Unless we organize ourselves to fight, they are going to continue to succeed in forcing kids into a life of torture and degradation.

Common Ground: The third component of human behavior that one needs to become facile with if you are going to be successful at motivating people to act, is that you need to be skillful at disarming opposition that may derail your efforts. We fail when we ignore how people perceive the issue and keep asserting our position. Then we get frustrated if we can't win them over to our point of view. Honestly, after listening to some of the objections people have given me regarding several social issues I want to slap them up the side of their head and exclaim, "What is wrong with you!?" Instead, I keep a neutral face and ask them, "why do you think that?" My willingness to listen encourages them to listen to me and helps me understand what I need to address. This is key to winning support for your cause.

For instance, there are many that feel that if we end hunger there will be a population explosion. This concern can be addressed by educating people regarding the cultural norms in the underdeveloped countries and why people there may have large families. One point Josette Sheeran makes in one of her blogs is: "When you provide food in schools, attendance skyrockets. If girls stay in school, they marry later and have smaller families." "The Blog" (Oct. 2010) The education of girls creates stronger families and the stronger the family, the less vulnerable they are to having their children become trafficking victims.

Understanding and utilizing the information in this section on how to create "common ground" will not only empower you to be more effective at fighting Trafficking; it will empower you in life because it addresses enrolling people in what you are doing who may not share your point of view. If you take on any project with groups, this is a skill worth mastering. Skillful leaders are able to get both sides together on an issue by finding out what both can agree on. They look for "common ground." (2.7)

When people oppose you, "Common Ground" is accomplished by validating another person's point of view. Then they feel heard and come receptive to what you have to say. Validating another's point of view doesn't mean you agree with them. It means giving the other person the sense that you do feel that their point of view is legitimate, that it has merit. If you do that they will be open to your point of view, even if they don't agree with you. This will create alignment which the group needs if they are to move forward. If someone in the group doesn't feel that they have been "heard," they will just become more assertive about expressing their point of view. The leader needs to validate them or the meeting will become a debate as to whose position is the "right" one. When people can't agree, resentment builds and pretty soon the group falls apart.

As a business consultant, when I was training people on how to do "conflict resolution" which is what this section is based on, I found that one of the most effective ways to train people in a distinction like this was to use an example that people were familiar with. Given that this book is written with a Faith based audience in mind, we are going to use the "Pro-Life/Pro Choice" issue as an example of how to create "common ground" because it is one that a Faith based audience is familiar with. It is a perfect choice to illustrate this distinction because it is so divisive. Faith Based groups are familiar with the Pro-Life argument, but oftentimes what is missing is skillfully giving people in the Pro-Choice camp the sense that their point of view has merit, so they will be receptive to what you have to say.

Some "Respect Life" groups assert that killing babies is evil. However many women who get an abortion in the first couple of months do not feel that they have killed a baby. Career women think that if they leave the "fast track" to have a baby, they will never achieve their goals. Poor, single mothers do not see how they can afford to take care of another child. Parents of teen girls want to protect their pregnant daughter from shame and make sure she goes to college and view her having a baby as interfering with that. They feel that their teen daughter is too young to be a mother and the grandparents "to be" feel that they are too old to take on adopting a baby. These are examples of the types of concerns one is speaking into when one is trying to encourage women to keep their babies and unless you address people's concerns they cannot *hear* you, no matter what issue you are trying to address.

So how do you validate someone's point of view when you absolutely do not agree with them?! You validate their commitment, not their position and trust that everyone wants the same thing, which is to have it all work. If you can show a group that, even if they are on opposite sides, you can create "Common Ground" and move forward. The Pro-Choice camp feels it is fighting for the woman. The Pro-Life camp feels it is fighting for the babies.

One of the best examples I have witnessed in creating "common ground" on this issue came in the form of a testimony at my church from one woman whose teenage daughter got pregnant. She shared authentically how once she and her husband got over the shock of finding out that their teenage daughter was pregnant, they sat down as a family and talked about how they could make it all work. They needed to figure out how the unborn child could be part of their family and still have her daughter go to college, etc. The grandparents "to be" felt that while they were too old to adopt a baby, they weren't too old to take on a six year commitment until their daughter was old enough and responsible enough to be a parent. That, they could do. However, it would take a lot of work and some sacrifice.

The grandmother shared how that little girl became the joy of her life and she misses her terribly, given that her daughter did grow up and got married so she only sees her granddaughter occasionally. She would take back all the work it took to be able to be with her granddaughter every day again. Her daughter can't imagine life without her child and is eternally grateful for her parents support in helping her with the baby until she did finish college. The whole experience bound them together as a family. What people are left with at the end of her share is perspective, opportunity and joy. She always has a crowd around her after the service asking her questions as many people know a teen that is pregnant. Her testimony had people who were considering having their teenage daughter abort, feel like they have been "heard," on this issue, that their concerns were legitimate. As a result they became open to considering another option.

Conclusion: With regard to Human Trafficking, what is often in people's way of taking action is their sense that it is happening in another country or community so they don't feel connected to the issue and they don't see how they can personally impact Trafficking. We can address these perceptions through education by quoting the stats for how prevalent Human Trafficking is for the city and country you are in. Even more powerful is to have a local group share the story of a victim who was exploited in the local community. At a presentation I did for Ministry leaders, there were volunteers there from the local "Crisis Pregnancy" center and they shared the story of a young girl who was being "pimped out" by her boyfriend. The center was located in the city where the ministry leaders lived, an affluent community. The participants were shocked and this story brought the issue "home" and created a sense of urgency for the participants to take action.

For some, another perception that is in their way of taking action on the sex trafficking side is that the whole concept of prostitution is distasteful. If truth be told, we don't like seeing known prostitutes come to our church services. In order to engage people in the fight we need to educate them to start seeing prostitutes as victims, kids who lacked family support, who often grew up with sexual abuse. They may have been tricked into the life, abducted or recruited when they were pre-teens or teens. What people see are prostitutes and people assume that prostitutes choose to make money by providing sexual favors. As a result, very young victims who were forced to work the streets as pre-teens, share that no one stopped to ask if they needed help.

The hardest part to keeping people motivated to keep fighting this issue, is that these kids who are being prostituted are invisible to the average person because most prostitution happens behind closed doors. With labor trafficking, for the most part we don't look closely at workers and assume that they are just like anyone else and can come and go as they please. As a result both sex and labor trafficking is "out of sight, out of mind," because we don't see it, even when it is right in front of us. We need to make the victims "visible."

A significant cultural shift that needs to happen, especially in the Third World, is the notion that woman are "property" or second class citizens. This perception justifies using woman as objects to satisfy one's desires and greed. Altering this perception and the sexual fantasy of being with a prostitute is critical to ending Trafficking.

The most likely victims are runaways and foster kids who are also "invisible." In addition, people often have a perception that street kids are "delinquents," drug addicts, irresponsible, etc. They don't want to help them because people don't want to deal with "delinquents." This is another perception that we need to address that is in people's way of taking action when it counts. There are ideas for how to do this in Chapter Six.

You may be thinking, how could everyone not agree to take action on this? Why include a section on "common ground?" The answer is that not everyone agrees on the kinds of action everyone should be taking. Your group may not agree on how to move forward. Law enforcement wants the NGO's (Non-Government Agencies) to have the victims they are working with, testify against the Traffickers. The victims are afraid to do that, so the NGO's don't contact law enforcement. This is an example of where law enforcement and the NGO's need to find "common ground."

Enough talk about the problem. Let's talk about the solution! With the resources available in our communities we have the ability to make people aware of what Human Trafficking looks like and to protect the most likely victims from hitting the streets and rescuing those who have. The "demand" side of sex trafficking is being fueled by porn addiction and if every Faith Group took on raising the kind of awareness recommended in the chapter on pornography, this addiction would be on the decline. The chapter on labor trafficking has many ideas for how to wake people up to stop purchasing products made by child and slave laborers. The goal of "Through God's Grace Ministry" is to inspire people around the world to establish a ministry or group at every place of worship or in their community to fight Trafficking. If we did that, we could end it.

By the time you are done reading this book, you will either know exactly what you can do or you will know where to start your research on finding out what can be done in your community using your unique talents and gifts. None of the actions by themselves will end Human Trafficking, but each one will chip away at the problem. If we engage enough people to "chip away," we will win the fight. In the words of Mother Theresa...... "I can do things you cannot, you can do things I cannot; together we can do great things."

References: (2.1)The Blog, Oct 10, 2010
(2.2) From the website "Mindreality.com/You-Create-All-of-Your-Reality-With-Perception."
(2.3) Statistic provided at meeting hosted by Focus on the Family for faith leaders to support their California adoption campaign.
(2.4) Book "Three Laws of Performance," by Steve Zafron and David Logan. "How a Situation Occurs Rises in Language."
(2.5) Yasmine Ryan, Jan 26th, 2011 "How Tunisia's Revolution Began." Aljazeera newspaper online.
(2.6) Testimony of victims.
(2.7) Conversation with a director of a "Respect Life" pregnancy center on her experience in working with organizations that work to create "common ground."

CHAPTER THREE

Let's Take Action!

This chapter and Chapter Four mainly address taking action to end sex and labor trafficking in the developed world. Chapter Five focuses on what we can do to end labor trafficking in the undeveloped countries. Before you begin any campaign to take action, first you need to take the time to educate yourself and purchasing this book indicates that you are aware of that. Once you have completed this book, you can follow our Facebook page "How You Can Fight Human Trafficking" to get updates on the information presented in this book. Once you type in the words, "Human Trafficking," you will get hundreds of pages, so just type in "How You Can Fight." Please do send us stories of what you are doing and we will post it.

Both "The Polaris Project" and "Homeland Security" sites offer great information, materials and videos you can use. To access the videos at www.dhs.gov, just search for "Human Trafficking videos." A truly great resource is the "In Plain Sight" podcasts at i-tunes and Stitcher which you can play on your phone. Each episodes interviews a key leader in the fight or someone just like you who is working to fight Trafficking. You will get great ideas. Another great series is the "Ending Human Trafficking" podcasts that are also at I-Tunes and Stitcher.

Another great way to educate yourself is to attend a Task Force meeting or a Conference or "Walk" in your area. Just google "Human

Trafficking Walk or Conference," (name of county, city or state). These local conferences or "Walks" can offer you networking opportu-nities with like-minded people who can tell you who is doing what in your area, like "Street Outreach," etc. The interactions you have at these events will energize and motivate you in the fight. If no one has a walk coming up, contact the group that sponsored the last walk in your area and ask them what groups are active in your community. Another place to find out what is happening locally is to contact Social Services and ask them if they have a group for Community Advocates that meets. While their focus is on foster care and adoption, these groups will often know who is working on Human Trafficking as foster youth are a target for the Traffickers. *(3.1)*

After reading "Victim" stories in books, many people's first emotional response is to want to go out and find a victim and rescue them. It is romantic and appeals to our desire to be a hero or heroine. However rescuing victims is really dangerous. A Trafficker would consider you to be stealing their property and they think nothing of hurting people. In addition, you may be interfering with the efforts of law enforcement. There was a concerned citizen group who tried to entrap a pimp, but they unwittingly interfered with a police sting and cost the city tens of thousands of dollars and ruined the case. While well intentioned, we need to leave law enforcement to the police. Our job is to call the police if we notice an underage kid being prostituted on the street or constant traffic to a hotel room or apartment. The kinds of actions in this chap-ter and the ones that follow are what will make a difference in the fight against trafficking that the average person can do with the emphasis throughout the book on prevention.

Become a Prayer Warrior

In order to end Trafficking, the world needs a conversion of minds and hearts and only God can do that. John Newton, author of the song "Amazing Grace" is a perfect example of this. John Newton was a slave trader who had given up the religious convictions of his youth. When faced with a violent storm at sea he prayed to God to save him. After being spared from death, John underwent a profound conversion and became a priest in the Church of England. He was instrumental in helping Wilberforce end slavery in that country. *(3.2)* The lyrics to his song profoundly express the conversion that the world needs in order to end slavery.

> Amazing grace! (how sweet the sound)
> That sav'd a wretch like me!
> I once was lost, but now am found,
> Was blind, but now I see.

Raise Awareness

Walks: You could invite your Rotary Club or Bible study, etc. to go walk down a main street in your city on a Saturday morning with your signs and flyers promoting the fact that Trafficking exists and on the sign let people know to call the 888 number to report trafficking. Your faith community can do a prayer walk. You can ask the police where in your city there are "Street Walkers." Walk down the street yelling "Our children are not for sale!" If the area is dangerous, invite the police to walk with you wearing their uniforms or drive by. If you want help organizing a "Walk" contact www.thea21campaign.org and you can join their nationwide effort to raise awareness through their annual "Walk." The feedback I have gotten from those who drove by most "walks" is that they didn't feel the "walk" had much impact because all it did was raise awareness that Trafficking existed. The people who drove by still did not know what action they could take, so think about a local action that you could promote.

Look around your community. Does your city have a 4th of July parade? If so, go to the "Polaris" website, print out their flyer and paste it to a stick. Invite your prayer group or MOPS (mothers of preschoolers), or men's group, etc. to march in that parade with your signs. Have flyers to give people regarding who is taking action in your area and pass them out when people come up to ask you what they can do.

Put out Flyers: Getting posters out is a great ways to raise awareness

We need flyers at all our transportation centers warning runaways that the Traffickers are looking for them.

so more victims know where they can get help and be rescued. "The National Center for Missing and Exploited Children," "Polaris," and the "Rescue and Restore" websites all have great flyers and information that you can download and hand out to your group. These posters can be put up at transportation centers like airports, bus and train stations, as well as truck and bus stops, liquor stores, emergency rooms and sexually oriented businesses. California just passed a law that makes it mandatory to post flyers where Trafficking victims might see them. No matter where you live, you can go to the California Department of Justice website for ideas as to where to put flyers up. Search for "Senate Bill 1193." (http://oag.ca.gov/human-trafficking/sb1193) At the very least, you should have a poster in the vestibule of your church , temple, etc.

Set up a Table: If you go to www.sharedhope.org and select "Join the Cause" at the top, it will take you to a page where you can select "Become an Ambassador." You can go to your local strip mall and ask the manager of a store there if you can set up a table and hand out flyers. You can set a table up on your college or high school campus or have a table outside at your place of worship one Saturday or Sunday. Shared

Hope International provides online training on domestic sex trafficking in the U.S. which will equip you to answer questions when people come up to your table to talk.

It costs money to make copies of a lot of flyers so I have two. One is from Shared Hope International on sex trafficking in the U.S. The other is a flyer that I put together with a list of local volunteer opportunities in my area, with a paragraph on the importance of buying "Fair Trade." You can find flyers from "Shared Hope" on the "Resources" tab. "Domestic Minor Sex Trafficking" is the one I use. On the table my group hosts are Fair Trade items like coffee, tea, sugar and a chocolate bar to educate people that while porn may create the demand for sex trafficking, we create the demand for labor trafficking through the purchases we make. People are under the assumption that because slave labor is illegal in their country that none of the products that they can purchase are made by slaves. It shocks people to find out that they are encouraging child and slave labor by something they do every day like drinking non Fair Trade coffee. (More on this in Chapter Five.)

The Sleep Out: A great awareness raising event is the "Sleep Out" that many youth groups are doing. In solidarity with homeless kids, the youth group participants sleep on the ground with only a piece of cardboard and their sleeping bag. That is it, no pillows or pad allowed. Covenant House offers a "Sleep Out" where participants sleep outside at one of the Covenant House facilities. The best part of this event is listening to the stories of how the youth wound up at Covenant House and how they turned their lives around. Their stories will enable you to inspire people in your community to take on these kids. You can find more information at their website under "Get Involved." Schools can duplicate this event as a way to raise awareness.

Become a Speaker: If you feel called to be a speaker, then you can email us at "ucanfightht@throughgodsgrace.com" and we will send you our power point that we use for presentations. You can use the handout that is at our site on the "Human Trafficking" tab and adapt both for your own use. If you want to show a short video, "Brianna's Story" at www.sharedhope.org provides a complete overview in less than 3 minutes of how teens get trapped into the life. This book will provide the foundation for anyone who wants to take on educating people on how to take action but you will need to make your talk relevant to the community where you speak by talking to the local police, social workers, community leaders, faith groups etc. Hearing the stories from those who work with victims and prosecute pimps will make this issue real for you and enhance your ability to speak. It will enable you to bring this issue "home" for people which needs to happen if you want people motivated to take action.

If you are Catholic and need a brochure you can get one at the "United States Conference of Catholic Bishops" site. (www.usccb.org) Search for Human Trafficking. Look for the entry on the list that has an Adobe Icon and download the brochure. The entry is entitled, "The movement of people across borders....." Religious orders can join "Talitha Kum" which has members from 71 countries. Catholic nuns are going on raids with the police and then taking care of the victims. Many orders have some project that is addressing Human Trafficking. www.talithakum.info

Faith Communities: A great resource for pastors and ministry leaders is Eddie Byun's book "Justice Awakening." He provides a prayer model that faith communities can utilize to fight trafficking, with biblical references that you can use at a meeting. Given that Trafficking is truly a great evil, it only makes sense for Faith Communities to take the lead in fighting this issue as it is only through the power of God will we overcome evil. The Office of Faith Based Partnerships in the U.S. is working with churches and sharing ideas of what other churches are doing. They are developing a curriculum that they are "field testing" which should become available sometime in 2015.

Host a Prayer meeting or a Discussion Forum at your place of worship. One church hosted a guest speaker who spoke on "How Can Men Prevent Human Trafficking." The event description let men know that they had a vital role to play and promised to show them pro-active steps they could take. Specific events are always more interesting than a general talk and you can promote your event to the local faith communities in your area.

If you have a working group, then share your group with other Faith Communities. Go visit pastors, rabbis, etc. in the churches, synagogues, etc. that are near to your faith community and invite them to your meetings or go out and speak to groups at your surrounding faith communities. Once people are shown a working model and are exposed to your enthusiasm and stories of the difference you are making, they will go start something where they worship. Locally, one church started a group entitled "Christian Coalition Against Human Trafficking." Fifty churches were represented at the first meeting. It was an opportunity to share what is working and not working and provided an opportunity to partner on projects which helps eliminate duplication in the community for activities. We need to mobilize our communities to act and at the end of this book, under "Supplement," is the outline of an outreach campaign to local churches that we do, that raises awareness among thousands in one day.

Create an Event or Conference: If you want to make it real for people that Trafficking is happening in your community, you could show the film "In Plain Sight." (www.inplainsightfilm.com) At the end you could have a local group share briefly and recruit for volunteers or raise money. The film has a companion study guide that could be used as part of a bible study entitled "In Plain Sight, Devotional and Group Study Guide." The (http://iempathize.org) group is doing a fabulous job of raising awareness and has great ideas for how to raise awareness at conventions, schools, etc. If you don't have the resources to do an event with speakers, music, video, etc., Iempathize has complete presentations with all the media you would need. They often have videos at their site that are available for you to download and use.

If your faith community wants to host a large event, then put out signs like Real Estate agents do, inviting people to a local park or your place of worship to come hear a speaker and answer questions. You can buy the posts to stick in the ground from a local shop that serves real estate agents and buy "cover stock" paper and print out what you want on the signs on your home printer. Most cities will let you put up signs for a day. You can ask them if you can tape signs to street posts. You will need to call your city as they will fine you if they have to tear down your signs because you left your signs up longer than the city allows.

Create a "Pastors/Rabbi/Inman/Faith Leaders" conference. Faith Leaders need to get together and dialog about this issue and get ideas from other faith leaders as to what they are doing that is working. Pastors are busy people, so you need to create urgency like inviting an intriguing speaker. In the U.S., you can contact the "Office of Faith Based and Community Partnerships" and ask for a speaker who can share ideas as to what other churches are doing. Since the speaker won't be local, it will be a "one time only opportunity," which will create the urgency you need. (http://www.whitehouse.gov/administration/eop/ofbnp)You can use the "Freedom Registry" or "Engage Together" to find local groups that could be part of a panel and also include law enforcement, social services, etc.   After an hour and a half, put everyone in groups for a "round table" discussion. Then invite people to stand up and share what came out of the "round table" discussions."   That is all you need for a powerful two and ½ hour event. Suggest that the pastors bring their ministry leaders as it is often the ministry leaders who will make the activities happen at their faith community.

You could do an event for school officials, teachers and youth pastors, where you invited the police, social services and probation ers. www.runawaygirl.org offers a training for this type of group. The program can address how to identify the signs of a child who is being trafficked, what kids are the most at risk, etc.   You could also include a facilitator from the "Enough is Enough" program or a speaker from www.fightthenewdrug.com on how to talk to kids about porn.   People who work with the youth need to understand what organization needs to intervene for each part of the Trafficking process and be educated on how a teacher or youth pastor would talk to a child who has become a victim.

There is mandatory reporting for teachers and youth pastors but mandatory reporting doesn't necessarily educate one on how to respond to a child who is terrified or thinks they are in love and needs to support their "boyfriend" financially. Pastors want to know what to do when a family approaches them because their child has gotten involved in trafficking or the child themselves steps forward. If they had someone at their faith community who knew what to do, like the youth pastor, they could facilitate and support that family.

Unique Awareness Raising Campaigns: Look around your community to find where you need to "wake people up." For instance if you live near a port, you can invite your friends or a men's group or a women's group or a prayer group to go down there and stage a prayer vigil for a couple of hours and invite the press. Create a banner with the 1-888-3737-888 number. You never know which dockworker you might have alerted to watching for women and kids being trafficked into the country. There may even be a worker there who may be a victim of labor trafficking whose rescue you might facilitate. Given that the docks may not be safe, it would be a good idea to bring a uniformed police officer with you.

Another unique way to raise awareness is to get your friends together and join the One Billion Rising event every year on Valentine's Day. (www.onebillionrising.org) This group has organized and coordinated men and women all over the world to dance on that day as a protest against violence to women. The You-Tube videos on this are awesome. They will fill you with joy.

Often a unique awareness raising effort or ministry was begun by people who took their own experience and started something. Harmony Dust started her organization by putting 3x 5 cards with biblical quotes on the cars of exotic dancers, letting the women know that in God's eyes they were more precious than rubies and gold. As a former exotic dancer, Harmony knew that the women did not feel good about themselves because of what they did, so she intuitively knew what to address. "Treasures" is now worldwide. If you ever have an opportunity to hear her speak, she would tell you to start with what you have, with what is in front of you. (www.iamatreasure.com) *(3.3)*

Zach Hunter started a unique project that teens across the country have now gotten involved in. Upon learning about Human Trafficking at the age of 12, Zach Hunter started a campaign to raise money for organizations that hired private detectives in the developing countries to-gather enough evidence to convict slave traders. In many countries, while Trafficking is illegal, the police will take bribes so the Traffickers can operate freely. His campaign "Loose Change to Loosen Chains" caught on at many schools and raised so much money that as a young teen, Zach was credited with saving thousands of women and children from becoming Trafficking victims. This is an outstanding project for any teen group to take on and you can find more information at his site.

How could you raise awareness right where you are at? How about a display at your college or annual church festival to promote Fair Trade. The PTA could host a table at the annual carnival with information on Fair Trade and information for parents so they can protect their children from becom- ing victims. You could encourage mall owners to host a "Heart Gallery" to encourage adoption at your local mall, given how vulnerable foster kids are to becoming trafficking victims. In one New York study, 85% of Domestic Minor Sex Trafficking Victims

"Heart Gallery" at a Mall to raise awareness regarding the need to adopt vulnerable kids.

had some contact with the Child Welfare System. In Orange County, California it was close to 90%. *(3.4)* It would make sense then, to do something in your community to raise awareness to recruit good foster/adoptive parents and mentors. (More on this in Chapter Six)

I shared with one church that the local police had shared with me that the Traffickers are on the beaches offering runaways jobs and then once the kid accepted the "job offer," they were taken out of the area and forced into the sex trade. So the group got a free table at the local farmers market at the beach, with a big sign that stated "Human Trafficking is happening in (name of city). At their table is information how Traffickers trick runaways, locations of Human Trafficking task force meetings, Fair Trade, etc. Where is trafficking most likely to be happening in your community? How could you raise awareness? Get creative and there is no end to the types of awareness raising events you could create.

Be a Community Activist

An Activist "Speaks Up: When the vulnerable are being exploited, an activist moves into action. Years ago, "Concerned Women for America" had a post about a well-known book store chain that started carrying a book that depicted little kids dressed provocatively, almost soft porn. A parent group decided that the books were not art and the people who were buying these books were not "Art Connoisseurs" so they asked the book store to take the book off their shelves. The book store refused in the name of "free speech" so the parent group went to the press and the local newspaper did an article on what the parent group was trying to accomplish. Within 48 hours of the news article hitting the stands, the books were pulled due to all the complaint calls the book store got. We need to watch for more of these types of books, videos, music lyrics, etc. and speak out against them.

Community Engagement: A great group that facilitates community engagement is "Oasis." They help organize the faith communities, schools, NGO's etc. in one city, to come together and identify what needs to be addressed in that community and what is missing in terms of services. So if beds are needed for victims, they might suggest having the faith communities work with "Run2Rescue" to create more housing for victims. They might suggest that Faith groups or schools provide the police with "Freedom Bags" to give to victims when they rescue them. Victims often come in with just the clothes on their back. The groups can all work together to create a conference to raise awareness. It is important to have these types of meetings to avoid duplication within the community, otherwise people in that community get confused as to who is doing what. The 888 number for Polaris can often let you know what organizations are operating in your area. Oasis has groups both in the UK and in the U.S. www.oasisusa.org and www.oasisuk.org.

Ask Your City to Put Up Billboards: The Orange County, California Human Trafficking Task Force partnered with the Orange County Transportation Authority for a BT1 (Be the One) campaign that entailed a wrap-around ad on the buses with the 1-888-3737-888 number to encourage people to report incidents of Human Trafficking. The Transportation Authority also trained its bus drivers on what to look for. Given that over 1 million people ride the bus every week, this is an impactful campaign.

Other cities are putting up "John" Billboards. (You can Google "John" billboards and "Human Trafficking" billboards to see what the billboards look like.) The problem is that while the "John" billboards may warn kids about the dangers of Human Trafficking, many of these kids will still have no place to go so they go with a Human Trafficker despite being warned, because they are hungry and cold and they have no other options. Other cities are putting up "Awareness" Type Bill-Billboards. In Los Angles, Metro.net/Rescue has one that states "Sexually Trafficked Children are Hiding in Plain Sight." ProtectOaklandKids.org has a billboard that is my all-time favorite which states: "Buying a Teen for Sex is Child Abuse. Turning a Blind Eye is Neglect."

Schools: After coming across Trafficking victims in her school, the Director of Guidance and Wellness for one school district took on driving the Traffickers out of her school. She created an information sharing system where social services, the probation department and the school shared information to identify the most likely victim. In 2010, before they had the information sharing system, 17 victims were identified. After instituting the system in 2011, 300 victims were identified! The youngest was 10. What is significant about this is that in identifying victims, they also identified their recruiters who were mainly other students. After identifying the recruiters, the police were able to find many of the traffickers who were then arrested. Many recruiters were told they could make $20 for every $100 dollars the victims made. Their most common ploy to enroll young women and boys into allowing themselves to becoming sexually exploited was to tell them, "you do it anyway, you might as well get paid for it." Here is the report: http://safesupportivelearning.ed.gov/sites/default/files/HumanTraffickinginAmericasSchools.pdf

As a result of all the arrests, social media blew up with posts referring to the fact that if you try and conduct the prostitution of minors out of that school district, you will most likely be caught so Traffickers are staying out of that school district. Those who were identified as recruiters were either arrested or expelled if there wasn't sufficient evidence to make an arrest. After the arrest, many students who were suspected to be recruiters transferred themselves out of the school. In every school district, we need to take a stand and drive the Traffickers out!

The involvement of minors as recruiters brings up an issue that many groups are becoming concerned with. In many ways, are they not similar to child soldiers? However, child soldiers get help. In the developing world, we prosecute recruiters. Just as we went from arresting prostitutes to now considering them be victims and getting them help, we need to consider the maturity level of a 13/14/15 year old boy or girl recruiter in considering appropriate consequences. However, we should not back off from increasing penalties for adults who are the clients and the Traffickers who are recruiting young teens to be recruiters and running the business of Trafficking minors.

Traffickers have told the police that it use to take nine months to trick a victim into the life. It now takes less than three months as a result of how sexualized the teen world has become. Magazines, music lyrics etc. are accomplishing the initial "grooming" stage which means making a potential victim more receptive to the idea of allowing themselves to becoming sexually exploited or to become a recruiter.

We all need to ask our school officials to please make a cyber-exploitation assembly and teacher training regarding how to identify victims, mandatory in the district. Many states have or will have regulations to provide education in schools. A great example of a project to raise awareness among students is the partnership between The National Consortium for Academics and Sports and UNICEF's End Trafficking project to create the "Shut Out Trafficking" program to raise awareness against human trafficking on ten university and college campuses. The week long program includes speakers, film screenings, appearances by prominent student-athletes and coaches, discussion groups with students and survivors of human trafficking.

I attended a presentation by the police regarding cyber exploitation. To make his point, the police officer went online and Googled "Jane, the soccer player," and found a picture of a 12 year old and then created a

We need to raise awareness at all schools for both parents and kids.

profile with the picture at a social networking site and used the name "Tracy." The police officer kept the site "live" and said, "just watch" and then continued on with his presentation. Within 5 minutes, "Tracy" had guys conversing with her. The police officer, who does this as part of his job, responded to them the way a 12 year old girl would. The third question from one of the guys was "Are you a virgin?" Then they began to describe their "equipment" and the conversation went downhill from there. It was devastating to the parents to think their young daughters would be exposed to such vulgarity. One mother burst into tears. The fathers wanted to kill.

The class or assembly for sex trafficking prevention needs to include the dangers of running away and all the tactics pedophiles and traffickers are using to trap kids in a nightmare. The kids need to be warned that the Traffickers can find out where one lives with the pictures one posts by utilizing geo-tagging. Showing the @3 minute "You Tube" video on geo-tagging has a real impact. The conversation needs to start at the middle school level or before. Teachers can ask Homeland Security to come speak or if they are unavailable, educators can go to the iGuardian site and utilize the materials there. There are geared for every age level.

The PTA can also order a complete presentation for @$27 entitled "Internet Safety 101 Multi Media Program" from www.enough.org and show it to parents. "Enough Is Enough" is one of the most respected websites to address this issue. The presentation was created in partnership with the Department of Justice. Enough.org has a facilitator's training and given how busy the police are, this may be a volunteer opportunity for you where you get trained and can present the program at schools. First you need to meet with the local police to find out how they want the public to work with them when a child is solicited by a recruiter or when one comes across a predator. If you are a facilitator I promise you this will be a question that will be asked, so you need to be prepared.

In my experience, you can really bring your program "home" by providing speakers who are former victims, someone the teens can relate to. www.sowerseducationgroup.com has speakers like this. They are located in Los Angeles and are raising awareness through schools. The A21 campaign (www.theA21campaign.org) is another great organization and provides a curriculum for educators worldwide. At the top of their page, select "Get Involved" and then scroll down to "Education." Once you register at the site, up pops the link where you can download "The Facilitators Guide," "Student Guide" and the videos.

Youth Groups: Our faith communities can do outreach by encourageing the teens in their youth groups to invite other teens to their meetings and activities. Some teens live in homes with drug addicted parents or are simply not getting enough attention, making them vulnerable to a Trafficker who *will* give them attention. Teens will often confide in their peers before they go to an adult. Most faith based youth groups do educate their teens on how to protect themselves, but those teens are most often from intact families. We need to reach out to the teens that are not part of a strong family so they can be included in the education process. Teens want to fit in so if chastity is an important value of that group and the teen likes the teens in the group, they will be more likely to practice chastity so they will be included by their peers. There are more suggestions for working with youth in Chapter Nine.

Malls: We need to ask mall owners to invite the police or Homeland Security to come do trainings for mall security. Given that teens hang out there, malls are a target for Human Traffickers to find teens. Anyplace that attracts teens needs to increase awareness among security and have them look for people who are soliciting teens in some way. If it "doesn't look right," security needs to investigate, not just make them leave the mall because they will just go to another mall. If the police take their name and that person keeps coming up as someone who is soliciting teens, then that will become a deterrent for a recruiter. A fabulous resource is the "Adopt a Mall" kit at the" Faith Alliance Against Trafficking and Slavery" site. Just go to their site and select "Take Action" at the right, then scroll down to "community" to find the kit. www.faastinternational.org.

Homeless kids will often station themselves at malls looking for other kids who will let them sleep on their couch. The kid with a back pack hanging out in the food court for hours is often a homeless kid. Think about it, a kid with a family does not often go to the mall with a backpack. The Traffickers know what these kids look like and are looking for them. It would be great if your church/synagogue/temple/mosque created a mall outreach and went and talked to these kids and helped them the way "Stand Up for Kids" does.

Reduce Cultural Messages that Encourage Demand: What about all the billboards that advertise for commercial sex oriented businesses like "Gentleman's Clubs" or "Men Only Spas" that advertise for "sensual massage." Lamar Advertising in Georgia is to be commended for changing their policy to stop advertising for these types of businesses. (3.5) Given that they own over 2/3rds of the billboards in Georgia, their action clearly hurt the efforts of the Traffickers to sell victims. It is not one action like this that will stop trafficking, but if everyone does their part, it will seriously cripple the commercial sex industry. As citizens, we need to do our part by asking businesses to take these types of actions.

Many parents are offended by how sexualized some store displays have become at their local mall. If you are one of them, then complain to the mall owner and let them know that you won't be going to their mall anymore because you don't feel comfortable walking through it with your young children. That will get their attention! What about being in a restaurant and hearing a song being played with graphic sexual lyrics. Write to the head of the company that owns the restaurant. Let them know you can't eat in a place that makes you uncomfortable. Companies do pay attention to these types of letters because statistically they know that one letter from a disgruntled customer often represents thousands who did not write. They can't afford to lose business over something as insignificant as playing music that offends people.

Get a group together and write to the media asking them to stop showing soap operas and other programs that show teens being promiscuous. Teens watch these programs and it reinforces the idea that "everyone is doing it." One parent group did a campaign years ago complaining about the fact that actors and actresses were shown with a drink every few minutes. If you notice, there is now very little alcohol and smoking in soap operas and TV shows. *(3.6)* If enough people write, it makes a difference. As part of their program, Sowers Education addresses cultural messages that teens are receiving through the media that makes them more susceptible to becoming victims.

We also need to ask the media to be more socially responsible and stop glamorizing pimps and prostitutes as part of sitcoms and other programming. Other than documentaries, often what TV programming shows is in sharp contrast to the reality of young female victims weeping in anguish as they relate the beatings, the terror, etc. of having been a prostitute. In talking to community leaders who are involved in fighting trafficking, over and over again they emphasized that in order to reduce the demand for prostitutes; we need for the media to address the fantasy of being with a prostitute. These girls and boys are not "hot" kids who "want it." They often are terrified kidnap victims. We need to work together to tone down how sexualized our society has become.

Massage Parlors: One can go to the Sports Section of newspapers and complain about the "massage" ads that the newspaper is running that may not be advertising for only massage. These ads have titles such as "Young and Beautiful Girls," with pictures of young and beautiful, scantily dressed women. True massage ads advertise a masseur's experience, like "10 years experience as a Swedish masseur." You can also go to websites and search for "Adult Services" and complain to those publications that are running ads that appear to be advertising for prostitutes.

"Massage ads and "Escort" ads are two examples of what Human Trafficking may look like that is happening in many communities. Are the "Escort" ads showing girls who look 14?" If they are, then complain to the newspaper and "Yelp" them if they aren't responsive. Be careful, though. You don't want to tell people that a specific massage parlor is a "front" for Human Trafficking if you don't know that to be true. Some people do want their masseur to be young and beautiful even if they are not looking for sexual favors. You don't want to undermine legitimate businesses as it is unethical to do that and you could be sued for slander. With that being said, stay alert. A local Chiropractic center in a "nice" area of town, offered massage as part of the therapy and patients were being solicited for sex. Sex trafficking can happen anywhere.

What happens in the massage parlors that are actually "fronts" for Human Trafficking is that the masseur will massage close to the erroneous zones. If the customer doesn't like that, then the "masseur" completes the massage. If the customer says something like "That feels good," then the "masseur" stops and asks the customer if they are a policeman. If the answer is "no," then they upsell them for various sexual favors. *(3.7)* If the customer goes to the police, it is the customer's word against the masseur's word. You could go as a group to the police and ask them if they want your help because if several people state that they had the same experience, then the police could make a case against the establishment. If you think a massage parlor is doing "back door" prostitution, then you should call the police and report it. If you think the police or a public official like a major, is profiting from these types of businesses or any incidents of Human Trafficking, then you need to call the Homeland Security Tip line. 1-866-DHS-2-ICE.

There are cities that have taken a stand against massage parlor prostitution by aggressively taking them to court. The thinking behind this is that if a massage parlor that will be offering "back door" prostitution, wants to set up business, they will avoid cities that are going to aggressively come after them. This is something you can encourage your city to do. If you are interested in taking on getting the illegal massage parlors out of your city, www.waronillegalpornography.com offers a plan to do that. Just go to the site and select "The Laws," at the top. On the next page, at the top right select "Opposing Local Sexually Oriented Businesses." This 149 page document has the kind of research an attorney or city needs to get started.

<u>Sporting Events, Shows and Rallies:</u> Thousands of women, many of whom are Trafficking victims, are brought into the Super Bowl and other major sporting events, car and motorcycle shows, etc. Covenant House has heard the stories from their rescued victims and share at their site that many Trafficking victims are part of a circuit that go from city to city where these events occur. You can distribute flyers about traffick-

ing hotlines to bars and hotels, where trafficking victims can see them. The Covenant House site posted the following for 2012 Human Trafficking awareness month.......''before the 2012 Super Bowl in Indianapolis, groups of nuns contacted the managers of 220 hotels and motels within a fifty-mile radius of the city and educated employees to recognize and report possible incidents of trafficking." (End of post)

This is a perfect example of a group organizing themselves to raise awareness where it counted. More and more groups are taking on raising awareness at major events. One example of this was the "It's a Penalty" campaign for the World Cup, 2014. A short film was shown on the planes going to the event, letting people know that having sex with a minor is a crime in Brazil. Participants were given a 100 number to call with the theme, "If you see something, say something."

In an FBI sting at the Super Bowl 2014, 46 pimps were arrested. Fifty women were rescued with 16 of the victims being juveniles, some as young as 13. The FBI reported that some of the kids had been reported missing by their parents. *(3.8)* Sharing these types of news reports will have people look at sporting events differently and put them on alert if they attend. We need more people calling the police when they attend these events if we want the Traffickers to stay away.

One Trafficking victim shared that the only time she had any privacy was in the bathroom. So Theresa Flores started a group that stamped soaps with the Human Trafficking hotline and text number and they put the soaps in all the bathrooms for sporting events and at all the surrounding motels and hotels. When they asked the surrounding motels if they would be willing to put them in their bathrooms, they gladly took them and told the group that they see Trafficking all the time and didn't know what they could do. You can find out more about Theresa's organization at www.traffickfree.com. You can hear her story on You-Tube.

So look around in your community for events where prostitutes will be brought in. Car and motorcycle shows can be huge. The motorcycle rally in Sturgis, South Dakota attracts over 650,000 riders and volunteers were there to raise awareness. This is an example of an event where a group could distribute flyers at any of the surrounding motels

You could raise awareness as to what products are created by slaves.

and hotels or set up a table at the event, letting the men know that the girls being brought in can be runaways, a victim of abuse, someone who could be their daughter. One faith group puts cards on the cars at these events with pictures of missing children asking people to look for that child among the prostitutes that are brought in. The cards make the point that the girls they see could have been abducted. Those cards have resulted in calls to the police and several children have been found this way. *(3.9)*

Community Outreach: Legal Organizations will sometimes do clinics in "at risk" communities where they meet with people to inform them of their rights or provide legal advice. In one instance, by listening to the stories people told, the volunteers picked up information that made them suspicious that Human Trafficking was occurring. They turned that information over to the police and arrests were made. This is one example of a community outreach activity that many organizations do that can result in arrests if the volunteers are educated as to what to look for and what to do if they think Human Trafficking is occurring. *(3.10)*

Advocacy: There are so many, many ways to be an advocate. You could invite your book club to make this book the next book they read. You could raise awareness regarding what products people are using that were created through slave labor. You could start a letter writing campaign to every coffee, electronics producer etc. and ask them to join the Fair Labor Association. (More on this in Chapter Five.) You can fight the demand for sex trafficking by doing a "White Ribbon" campaign at your place of worship and include letter writing at your table to the attorney general asking him/her to be more aggressive about prosecuting porn producers. You could go to your county and ask them to get porn out of your libraries. (More on this in Chapters Seven and Eight.) You can go to your schools and encourage them to do teacher training on how to recognize victims. You could go to your city council meeting and ask them if they are including "What does trafficking look like?" as part of their "Neighborhood Watch" program. You could ask them to do what many cities are doing, which is post the picture and name of the clients (AKA known as the "paying rapists") at their website. You could ask your Post Office to have Homeland Security provide training for their mail carriers. You can go to all the places where teens hang out like malls, swap meets, the movies and ask them to make sure they are providing training to their security team regarding what to look for and what to do if they find teens who are being solicited. You can use social media to raise awareness by sending links to videos that many websites offer. Throughout this book are many suggestions for advocacy.

Part of the job of supporting any organization that you or your group chooses to support, is to find out what types of advocacy they need and go talk to your representatives about it. At Task Force meetings, conferences and "walks" you can find out about groups that may be working on legislation. The Trafficking Victims Protection Act of 2000 is an example of churches, NGO's and lay groups working with government to get laws passed to protect victims who were afraid to come to the police for fear of being deported. People involved in supporting groups who help foster kids were made aware of the need to extend benefits to kids past the age of 18. So they went out and fought to have foster kids benefits extended to age 21, if they stay in school or are enrolled in a work program. This is an example of advocacy that protects kids from being trafficked.

A great site to get information regarding what to advocate for is www.castla.org. Even if you don't live in California, their suggestions are worth considering for every state. Select "What You Can Do" and scroll down to "Take Action, Support Legislation." The "Shared Hope International" site also includes a section on current bills. The Covenant House site offers opportunities for advocacy under the "Get Involved" tab. Scroll down to "Be an Advocate." Throughout this book are letter writing opportunities that you can take on. Raising money is another way to be an advocate, as all fundraisers raise awareness for the cause one is asking donations for.

Labor Trafficking

Look Around Your Community: Are the people at your local nail salon working 12 to 16 hour days? When you go visit your mother or father at the local retirement home, are the same people there every single day? If you ask an employee "How are you" and the person seems fearful and quickly leaves the room, you should be suspicious. Go say "hi" to the other people working there. Do most of the employees seem fearful?" If so, you should call the hotline. What about the dishwashers at your local restaurant? Does it seem like they never have a day off?

At one presentation that I did, a woman told me that she did notice that the people in her mother's retirement home did not seem to have a day off, so she asked one of the workers there about his hours. He told her that everyone there was required to work double shifts, so she asked me what she should do. I told her to call Polaris and ask them because the worker may have been told to say that. An agent with Homeland Security who was doing the talk with me agreed. If it doesn't "look right" or "sound right," make the call. 1-888-3737-888.

What about your neighborhood? With all the awareness that is starting to be raised regarding Human Trafficking, my friend took in a foreign exchange student and her neighbor came over and talked to the girl to make sure she wasn't really an illegal domestic servant that could be a slave. My friend commended her neighbor for being willing to risk possible embarrassment to protect a child.

The rescue of Shyima Hall is a case in point where a neighbor was responsible for the rescue of a child. Shyma was born in Egypt, the seventh child of desperately poor parents. When she was eight, her parents sold her into slavery. At the age of ten, she was smuggled into the U.S. and was rescued two years later when a neighbor, who could see her through the window, noticed Shyima never went to school and called the police. Shyima was forced to work 18 hours a day, 7 days a week as a very young child. Her book "Hidden Girl," tells her story. What struck me the most after hearing her story was how alone she was. She had no friends and no one ever asked her how she was and she was a little girl! Her story is compelling. *(3.11)*

References: (3.1) State of Human Trafficking in California 2012 report
(3.2) "Amazing Grace: The Story of John Newton" by Al Rogers.
(3.3) Harmony Dust, Saddleback 2014 ,HumanTrafficking conference.
(3.4) Presentation by Orange County DA at the Human Trafficking panel for the Travel Industry hosted by the Jr. League. 5.16.14
(3.5) The book "Not in My Town" by Dillon Burroughs and Charles Powell
(3.6) Conversation with a friend who was part of the Hollywood wives group that took on this campaign
(3.7) One man's personal blog who did not provide his name
(3.8) The New American, Feb 4, 2014, Super Bowl Sting Rescues 16 Juveniles, 50 Women From Sex Trade
(3.9) Volunteer who was part of the group who distributed the cards with the pictures of missing children
(3.10) Example from Ending Human Trafficking podcast #72, Vanguard University, Costa Mesa
(3.11) Shyma's talk at the Vanguard 2014 Human Trafficking Conference "Why is She a Slave?" 3.08.14

CHAPTER FOUR

Actions for Volunteers and Special Groups

Y ou can find a local group to volunteer for from the Salvation Army and other organizations that are involved in fighting this issue. You could join a club like the Soroptimist Club or a council like the National Council of Jewish Women with their Exodus project and partnership with Polaris. I meet a lot of people who have a great idea and want to start a non-profit. I would recommend looking around your area and joining an organization that has experience and support what they are doing and work with them to include your idea. This is not a simple issue. It can take years to truly understand all the dynamics and how to best proceed with your idea. By joining an already existing organization, it provides more focus for your community, instead of everyone's efforts getting diluted by scores of organizations that are doing similar work and competing for grants.

Recruit for Volunteers: You can go meet with your local organizations like a runaway hotline, "The Salvation Army," "Big Brothers and Big Sisters," "The A21 Campaign," "Florida Coalition against Human Trafficking," the "Chicago Alliance Against Sexual Exploitation," etc. directly and get ideas from them regarding how to promote them or volunteer for their "awareness raising events." If you are a "sales" type you could go to an orientation to learn how to answer basic questions and offer to be an advocate for that organization.

Engage Together (www.engage-together.org) has a program similar to a "Match.com." On the "Engage" tab, organizations that are fighting trafficking sign up and create a profile regarding what they need in terms of volunteer help. On the same tab, individuals sign up and create a profile and based on that profile, they will match you up with a local organization that needs what you have to offer in terms of talents or desire to serve. It is a brilliant tool to mobilize a community.

Contribute your Talents: What are your gifts? Jon Klein and Chris McCarley used their hair cutting skills to develop teams to go around the world and teach rescued woman a trade. They formed "The Trade Foundation" and partner with Agape International, a worldwide rescue organization.

I was at a barbecue and mentioned the fact that I wrote this book and people's comments were pretty much along the line of "good for you." No one asked where they could get the book. Then later we were talking about health and I mentioned the fact that I eat organic on a budget and for years people had been telling me that I should write a book entitled "15 Minute, Healthy Organic Meals for Less Than $10 a Day." Eight out of ten people at the table said "I want that book!" Given that the health market is a much larger market than the number of people who are interested in finding out how they can fight Human Trafficking, I decided to write the book and show people how to incorporate Fair Trade food products as part of their meal planning. While the "food" book delivers on its promise of showing one how to eat organic on a budget in a way that saves time, I am now reaching thousands to raise awareness regarding labor trafficking and climate change which is impacting our food supply and the poor. I am sharing this because many of you have a talent or gift. How could you use that gift in a way that promotes awareness and encourages people to take action like my example and that of Jon and Chris.

Most local organizations have volunteer orientations or information online so you can find out how to volunteer. However, you don't need to always offer to volunteer for what is on the list. You can meet with them and offer your special talents. Are you great at "social media?" The book "Twitter for Good" makes the case that all non-profits need a Twitter account. They all need to maintain a Facebook page. Very few non-profits have the funds to hire a person to do this, so this is something you could contribute. Sales types are usually very good at recognizing "marketing" opportunities like the example above for Traffic Courts. If you have a creative idea, suggest it!

Create a Task Force: What is really making a difference is when counties or cities create a task force that meets monthly. Task Forces are a powerful way to create strong networks. Who is invited are the public, law enforcement and community organizations that are involved in the fight. Who shows up are Homeland Security, local law enforcement, pregnancy centers, rehabilitation groups, faith leaders, health professionals, etc. The reason why pregnancy centers are at the meeting is because prostitutes do go there to find out if they are pregnant. Pregnancy centers are beginning to recognize that they are seeing victims of Human Trafficking and want to be educated on what to do. These meetings have a speaker and then break up into groups where each group shares what is working in the area where they work. Those who provide awareness and education are one group. The organizations that work with victims are another group. Law Enforcement is another group. Faith Communities are another group.

These task forces allow different groups to contribute to each other. At one task force meeting, a rehabilitation organization met with law enforcement and let them know that when they "cuff" the 15 year old, in her mind you do not see her as a victim, you see her as a criminal. As a result, she will be less responsive to supporting Law Enforcement in prosecuting her pimp. The pimps have already brainwashed her into thinking that Law Enforcement is the enemy and "cuffing" her reinforces that perception. Law Enforcement "cuffed" prostitutes because up until recently, they were all looked at as someone who was breaking the law, so that was a part of their procedure. Given that we are now considering all minors as victims, "cuffing" is no longer appropriate. Neither is referring to them as "prostitutes." We need to refer to them as "victims" and reinforce that thinking for them as many do not see themselves as victims. They consider themselves to be "girlfriends" of their pimp and a "girlfriend" protects her "boyfriend." It was also suggested that we refer to the clients as "Paying Rapists." Calling them "Johns" is disarming because "John" sounds like a regular guy and since perception influences one's actions, we don't want the public considering a man who rapes women a "regular guy." The education that happens at these monthly meetings is invaluable and a task force can be started by any group who has influence in the community.

NGO's and law enforcement have started Task Forces. Locally one was started by "Kingdom Causes, Long Beach," a faith-based non-profit organization that had been working for years to build cross-sector collaboration, city-wide to activate the gifts of the neighborhoods and city for positive change. This group already had the trust of the community and community partnerships, so they had the connections needed to reach out to the different groups in their community to build a Task Force. Mega churches often have these kinds of connections. We need to do whatever is possible to build networks to fight. When our networks are stronger than those of the Traffickers, we will win!

Take a Vacation: What does your community need? If it is not offered locally, then take a vacation and go spend a week finding out how a group works in another city or take a "tour" of several organizations in different cities. If your community needs street outreach to homeless kids, them come to San Diego, California and ask "Stand up for Kids" to train you and then go back and start a chapter. They will post your chapter at their site so local people can find you. What about street outreach? You can go with xxx.church when they do porn conventions and hand out material. You can ask Annie Lobert to train you in the street outreach that she does and go to Las Vegas to learn how she works. Afterwards you can watch a show and lay around by the pool. You can find out more about "Hookers for Jesus" in the chapter on street outreach.

All the central state or county organizations like CASTLA.org, the Florida Coalition Against Human Trafficking, etc. offers several trainings. You can come lay on the Los Angeles or Florida beaches and go to a training and bring that information back to your group or faith community. While you are in Southern California, you can come to an Orange County Human Trafficking Task Force meeting and/or contact www.live2free.org and/or The A21 Campaign and get trained on how they do presentations to High Schools and learn how they are getting college kids involved in the fight.

Internships: Many, many organizations need interns. You just need to ask. If you are an "advocate" type, contact "The A21 Campaign" or the "Chicago Alliance Against Sexual Exploitation" or other organizations like this. If fighting porn is your passion, you can intern for Porn Harms.com. Organizations that take care of victims and street kids need interns. Covenanthouse.org offers a one year program for college students to serve homeless kids full time. You can learn what they do and bring that back to your faith community and help them set up a program for homeless youth. At their site, select "Get Involved" and scroll down to "Faith Communities." This organization is always adding programs, so visit their site from time to time to find out what may be available.

Do you feel that God is calling you to rehabilitate victims? Then ask the police who is doing that in your community or a surrounding community and ask your faith community to sponsor you to go work for them as an intern. You could work with the Dream Center's victim rehabilitation program and live there for year and get trained and bring what you learned back to your faith community. "The Dream Center's" outreach programs completely and totally transformed their local community. Learning about this Center's programs would be an adventure!

Faith Communities: Faith Communities can find out what volunteer opportunities local organizations need and recruit for them and do fundraisers for them. They can also form community partnerships and offer their resources. www.engage-together.org has developed an outstanding toolkit that faith communities, service organizations, etc., can use to facilitate them in collaborating with each other within their community. Kids who are coming out of group homes or the probation department are often kids without families. Churches can partner with Social Services and invite these kids who want to get on the "right track" to your churches "singles group" or a bible study. No one does very well on their own. We all need a community to be part of. There are more suggestions for actions like this in the chapter on "Start a Group."

<u>Volunteer in Another Country:</u> Many of you feel called to help victims of both sex and labor trafficking in the Third world. David Batstone's book "Not For Sale" will inspire you how people are using their gifts to make a difference around the world. If you are former navy seal, military or SWAT, recue organizations like "Justice Be Done" need you for rescue operations. There are lots of great "rescue and rehabilitation" groups like "Destiney Rescue" that you can volunteer for in the Third World. Most Faith Groups have their own groups that are doing amazing work. The "International Justice Mission" works with "Rescue" groups to prosecute the Traffickers and "root out" the corruption that fosters trafficking. If working in the Third World is on your heart, then be courageous and at least find out what is involved in becoming a volunteer. At the Vanguard Human Trafficking Conference 2014, Dr. Joanna Butrin, Director of Assemblies of God Missions, shared that ¾ of the women her group worked with credited their faith as giving them the strength to leave prostitution. Faith and prayer are important weapons in the fight.

Professionals

<u>Parents:</u> There are two categories for this. The first group are the ones whose children have not been trafficked. The second part of this section is for parents whose children are currently or have been trafficked. While not considered a "professional," parents need to educate themselves, much like any professional does, on how to protect their children from exploitation. Parents need to look through their children's media to eliminate music and games that glamorize "pimp" culture and the abuse of women such as the games where one can get a lap

dance or stop their car and go beat up the prostitute on the corner. Traffickers are using Social Media to entrap kids into becoming victims so we need to monitor their internet use. A great book to educate parents on everything their child might be into is "Seduced, the Grooming of America's Teenagers" by Opal Singleton.

The Traffickers have a whole curriculum for their recruiters on how to trick teens, what to say, how to act understanding, etc. At one Human Trafficking presentation, "cyber cop" provided two critical statistics. The first one was that 100% of victims who were recruited through the internet went willingly. (100% is not a typo!) That is because they think they are meeting up with someone their age who is attractive and understands them. The second statistic was that there is a correlation to the number of family dinners per week to a child's mental health. A child whose family spends time with them over dinner is a child who feels valued and is less likely to be trafficked.

Given that the recruiters play on a teen's frustration with their parents, your best defense as a parent is to take parenting classes on how to avoid the manipulation of teens, so you can be there for them instead of resenting and avoiding the ones that can be difficult. Parents can take advantage of programs that teach them how to protect their children from being solicited online, like the "Enough" program does. They can watch the www.netsmartz.org videos together with their children.

The Traffickers aren't responsible for making sure the teen gets their homework done, etc. so their job of validating a teen is easy. During the "grooming" process they never broach a subject that will have them wind up in an argument with the teen. They are great actors and actresses and will agree with everything the teen says, especially how you, the parent makes their life so difficult and how you can't even begin to understand your teen. However the "Romeo" pimp completely understands your teen and how frustrating and difficult their life is and that a teen just wants to have fun. So they make sure the teen is always flattered and has fun when they are with them and constantly validate how much they love them. *(4.1)* Many convince the teen to run away with them by telling them they can have fun all the time and avoid all your restrictive parental rules. Running away gives the Trafficker complete control.

One 17 year old from Portland fell in love with a guy online who she thought was 20, from a rich family and going to college in New York. He told her that he couldn't Skype because his computer did not have a camera. That should have been her first clue but it is human to trust people we love that we think love us. He told her how to purchase a phone that did not have tracking capabilities and convinced her to run away to come live with him and his family, to escape her "horrible" home life. She was met by the police in New York due to the quick action of her mother who was closely monitoring her daughter. *(4.2)*

The main goal of the recruiter/pimp is to have the teen fall in love with them and they are very good at this. Once that happens, then the "Romeo" pimp claims that they need money for something, like an operation that will save them from death. (Don't laugh, this has been done.) All the teen needs to do is to have sex with a stranger to help them get the money. Of course, the teen will do anything for the man they love! Convicted "Romeo" pimps have told law enforcement that once they are successful at getting the teen to have sex once with a stranger, after that it gets very easy to "pimp them out" on a regular basis.

I am including all this here, because "forewarned is forearmed." Teaching your teens how teens get tricked is important. Theresa Flores shares in her You-Tube video that all the bells were going off in her head, warning her that she should not go with the good looking guy. Then he said three words...."I like you." After that, she ignored all the bells and wound up a Trafficking Victim. *(4.3)*

Parents Whose Children Have Been Trafficked: There are two support groups that I know of. If you don't have a support group in your area, you might want to contact F.A.S.T. Families Against Sex Trafficking. (http://families4fast.org) Another great one is "Mothers Against Trafficking." There is more than one group with this title, but the one I am referring to is run by Heather, who paid the pimp her daughter's quota so she could visit with her. Those visits resulted in her daughter being re-united with her family. Most people are shocked to learn that prostitutes are so brainwashed by their Trafficker, that even if a family tells their son or daughter that they love them and want them back, they don't believe them. Heather let the pimp know that she forgave him for what he did to her daughter and he confided in her that many pimps want to get out, but are addicted to the money. Her daughters pimp did "get out" as a result of how moved he was by Heather's forgiveness. Heather stresses how important it is to not give up on our children when they disappoint us by becoming drug addicted or are lured into prostitution. You can contact her at mothersagainstht@gmail.com.

Hotels and Motels: Many cities are passing ordinances that prohibits motels and hotels from renting rooms by the hour. They are also encouraging them to block porn. We need to create the perception for the Traffickers that they can't hide, so Trafficking becomes a bad idea to get involved in. It would be great if we could get every hotel and motel, every airline, every bus and train station etc. to put up a poster to the effect of.... "Human Trafficking NOT Tolerated Here. $500 reward for any tip that results in the conviction of a Human Trafficker. If you think you may be a victim of Human Trafficking, call 1-888-3737-888." The reward money could come from the assets that are seized when the Traffickers are convicted. This would be another example of local government working with businesses to fight trafficking and we need partnerships like that if we are going to win.

However, in talking with hotel management, especially high end hotels, they tend to be reluctant to do something like this because they don't want their guests to think trafficking might be happening in their hotel. However, they are willing to let the police put out a flyer that they might keep somewhere near the front desk. Then the perception of the public is that the police are just doing their job to raise awareness everywhere and this is not necessarily something that, that hotel is concerned about.

www.ECPATUSA.org is the leading policy organization fighting the Commercial Sexual Exploitation of Children for the travel industry. ECPATUSA has developed a code of conduct that every airline, hotel, etc. can model. Any hotel/motel employee can ask their management to sign "The Code" which is a commitment to be vigilant about reporting cases of child abuse. The commitment needs to be expressed in employee training as to what actions to take. Employees for these businesses need to call the police if they see "clients" coming and going all night. They need to be educated on scenarios that are suspicious like a room that is asking for towels every hour and who answers the door is a 14 year old.

A great outreach activity for a faith group or women's group etc. would be to contact owners of hotels and motels in your area and educate them about "The Code" and the need for training their employees. You can find a list of hotels and motels that have signed the code at ECPAT.org. Even if the hotel/motel has signed it, your group can ask them if they are expressing that commitment by providing training on "recognizing what Human Trafficking looks like and how to respond."

Your group can also ask them to block all porn to their rooms. If they signed "The Code" but are showing porn, they are throwing water on the fire on one side and gasoline on the other. That is not to say that if there was no porn, prostitution would not exist but many sites like "The Christian Broadcasting Network" will tell you that we have a porn pandemic. Porn addiction has created a demand for sex slaves and prostitutes that never existed before online porn became available. For the hotels and motels who are protecting kids, we can "Yelp" and promote them. If they are contributing to the problem, we can "Yelp" and express our concern.

We can also ask our faith communities and the companies we work for to only book their traveling salespeople and executives at "porn free" hotels and motels that have signed "The Code" and to use the same criteria if they are booking a conference. We need to "vote" with our dollar. Hotels and Motels do not want to lose business and they will make changes if the public puts enough pressure on them to do that.

Attorneys: There is a real need for legal services for victims. To start, attorneys can get involved with organizations like CAST. They have a working group for attorneys to ask questions or share information about handling Human Trafficking cases. (www.castla.org) Even if you are not handling cases, but want to raise your own awareness on the legal side, you can join their conference call by contacting "attorney@castla.org" or you can take their "Human Trafficking 101 course." Select "Resources and Training" and scroll down to legal resources.

What is really needed is for the legal community to create networks of legal service providers to assist the NGO's who are providing assistants to victims. A Christian organization for attorneys like the Christian Legal Society (www.clsnet.org) or the St. Thomas Moore society could add a page to their website where attorneys could post their expertise and NGO's can find them. As more and more awareness is raised regarding this issue, more and more attorneys will want to help but they will need a network to be part of.

Law Enforcement: The Rescue and Restore website has great information (www.acf.hhs.gov/programs/endtrafficking/partnerships) for Law Enforcement. Just click on "Toolkits." Homeland Security's Blue Campaign is another great resource. You can search at any state's Department of Justice site and find information as to what is being done in that state. Peace Officers can take a Post Training course on how to identify victims, collaborate with victim resource providers and how to develop human trafficking cases. These courses have become mandatory in many states.

"The State of Human Trafficking in California, 2012" report outlines the ways that law enforcement is being facilitated to become more and more technology savvy with regard to how the Traffickers are using the internet to "market" kids. Conferences are being created for law enforcement, NGO's etc. Technology experts are working to create tools to create more efficiency in fighting this crime. You can find out who these groups are in the Trafficking report and join them if this is your area of expertise. Social Media sites are working to support law enforcement, however we need to keep asking them to "step up" their efforts and aggressively report offenders, not just take them down from their sites. You can find the guidelines for Facebook "Safety" by going to: http://facebook.com/safety/groups/law/guidelines.

<u>Health Professionals, Teachers and Youth Pastors:</u> This group is on the front line and has a special role to play. For that reason Chapter Nine in this book has been devoted to the actions they can take. Even if you are not a member of this group, you can do your part by reading the chapter and raising awareness with the teachers, health professionals and youth pastors that you know.

<u>Flight Attendants:</u> The AAI website features the following story of Nancy Rivard, a flight attendant who took action when "things did not look right." During a flight home from a conference for Airline Ambassadors, where she had taken a workshop on Human Trafficking, Nancy noticed a woman traveling with a little boy and girl. The girl was sobbing and both children seemed very distressed and the woman did not even seem to know the names of the children. So Nancy called the hotline number she had gotten at the workshop. As a result 82 children who had been brought to the U.S. illegally from the Dominican Republic were rescued. Nancy then took on educating her fellow flight attendants. Airline Ambassadors International (AAI) offers training for airline and airport support personnel. Their Facebook page is really impressive.

<u>Truck Drivers:</u> The trucking industry has recognized that truckers can be instrumental in fighting Trafficking so this industry is taking this issue on. One example is the Montana Motor Carriers Association partnering with the Montana Attorney General to put 200 posters on trucks at the Montana Truck Driving Championship, to raise awareness. *(4.4)*

In response to the abuse that is happening at truck stops in the U.S., Kendis Peris took it upon herself to raise awareness by starting "Truckers Against Human Trafficking." She saw a need and went to work. TAT partnered with "Iempathize" to make a video of the story that was told in Chapter One of the two cousins who were rescued from a truck stop and they show that video at Trucking Conventions. At the conventions, the Truckers share that they have daughters and granddaughters and they want to help and TAT gives them actions to take. TAT has a website and a hotline to help members of the trucking and travel plaza industries to identify and report instances of human trafficking. *(4.5)*

What Kendis did is one of the main themes of this book which is.......

*Truckers against Trafficking is featured in the United
Nations "100 Best Practices" report.*

"use the talents you have for the community you are familiar with to raise awareness as to what actions people can take." TAT is one of the stories featured in the UN report "100 Best Practices in Combatting the Trafficking of Persons, the Role of Civil Society." The report is at www.ungift.org, which stands for "UN Global Initiative to fight Trafficking." The report will inspire you as to what people are doing around the world and give you many ideas as to what you can do. Just type "100 Best Practices" in the search box.

<u>Business Owners and Corporations:</u>   If you are a busy entrepreneur who has no time to help, know that you are actually a leader in the fight against Human Trafficking and most other social issues because at the root of almost every social issue is lack of economic opportunity. If you are providing jobs for people you are doing your part. Many groups like "Not for Sale" (www.notforsalecampaign.org) are connecting with community partners to create jobs for survivors and "at risk," low income youth. Their latest project is entitled "Reinvent: Bay Area." We need more community projects like this.

Lack of employment is causing people to migrate. Immigrants are often taken advantage of by criminals. In addition, the migration will often break up families and these families become targets for Traffickers. One of the root causes for domestic violence is the lack of meaningful employment that a man feels will earn him respect. Respect is very important to men and when they don't have it, the frustration can be overwhelming leading to alcoholism, spousal abuse, etc. Children who are part of a domestic violence situation or any situation that lacks family stability are vulnerable to becoming exploited in some way. (4.6) Your willingness to provide company training, so people have upward mobility is doing your part to create meaningful employment.

One of the attractions of gangs is that they offer men and boys jobs that provide them with the respect that they seek. While the respect may only be coming from other gang members, for a boy or man the experience of respect can be addicting which is one of the reasons why gangs have such a hold on so many kids. Now that gangs have made Human Trafficking one of their money making ventures, employing former gang members would be doing your part. (4.7) Organizations like Covenant House are also looking for jobs for former street kids.

You could also be a speaker for those groups that are working with "youth at risk" and educate gang members and former street kids on how to be successful at getting what they want. Many gang members have children and families to support and they can't see their way to taking care of their families unless they make money with the gangs. As entrepreneurs you can show them another way.

Men

Fathers: Fathers have a very important and special role in the fight. Police who work in Special Victims units will tell you that the way to make your daughters less vulnerable to becoming a Trafficking victim is to validate how beautiful they are, that you love them. If the first time they hear those words is from someone who wants to exploit them, those words will fill a hole in their heart and they won't be able to get enough of it.

Fathers need to be educating their daughters as to how boys view girls who are "easy." While the "easy" girls may be getting a lot of attention and seem popular, if these girls knew how teen boys talked about them behind their backs, they would rethink their actions. Girls who are already sexually promiscuous become easy targets for Traffickers. Men also need to be role models for their sons on how to treat women. It would make a difference if fathers taught their sons that prostitutes are real people, women who were most likely exploited.

Male Leaders: Men in leadership roles like boy-scout leaders can incorporate many actions in this book. Boy Scouts of America are encouraging their leaders to show the Netsmartz videos produced by "The Center for Missing and Exploited Children" to protect boys from being solicited online. We need to ask our Boy Scout groups if they are doing that and we need the Boy Scouts to address pornography and a young boy's view of women. I know some men feel awkward talking about this because they themselves looked at Playboy, Hustler, etc. when they were young, but there is a qualitative difference on the brain from looking at pictures in Playboy and watching videos. When one watches videos, we project ourselves in the story. Any activity done over and over again, like watching porn, creates neuro-pathways in the brain. A boy's brain, particularly when it comes to considering long term consequences is not fully developed until 24, so we have young boys who are acting out what they see with younger siblings. (See chapter on pornography.) Teens become addicted to pornography very easily.

Ministry to Men Who Use Prostitutes: The best speaker I have heard on how we are to respond as Christians regarding men who use prostitutes is a speaker from www.mstproject.com. This group goes out to "Red Light" districts to talk to men. They are awesome! The MST Project should be represented at any Human Trafficking conference because while all conferences address the victimization of women, very few address the victimization of men. This aspect of the issue needs to be addressed in order to reduce the "demand" side of Trafficking. One of their mottos is "We choose to open our arms instead of pointing our finger." Another is that "Men are part of the solution."

The speaker for the MST project made several points. The main one is that many men go to prostitutes looking for love, value, and intimacy – deep issues of the heart. One man told the MST group that "He didn't have any love in his life, so he was willing to pay for it." He knew it wasn't real, but it was all he thought he had available to him." Many men seek prostitutes for the same reason that others use drugs or alcohol or food. It is all a symptom of brokenness. Telling these men that they are perverts only has them feel bad about themselves. The speaker claimed that telling men that won't change the behavior for many of them. *(4.8)*

Another point this group made is the emphasis by the media and advertisers on "pleasure," so people seek "pleasure" to reduce stress, boredom, etc. Food addiction, men utilizing prostitutes, etc. can be the result of the search for pleasure. However sensory pleasure is fleeting. It is only in seeking the true joy of the Lord will we ever be satisfied. Having a cause, knowing that you made a difference in someone's life can really "light one up," and fill the void one may have instead of using sex, food, etc. to do that.

There are many men who may only occasionally have a girlfriend. Their need for love may need to come from a different source, like a church group that they belong to. While not the same as having an intimate relationship, support and affection from a group can be fulfilling and help alleviate the pain of loneliness that many men use prostitutes to escape from. MST stands for "Men and the Sex Trade" and is made up of men ministering to other men. This group will do trainings in your city if you would like to start a chapter.

Men's Groups: There are many, many men's groups that one can get involved with at almost all places of worship. There are many nationwide groups that are taking action, like www.joinonemillionmen.org who have taken on supporting other men in becoming porn free. Another site is Shared Hope International, where one can sign the pledge to become a Defender. Other groups like Menapat, which stands for "Men Against Prostitution and Human Trafficking" took on a campaign to force social media sites to eliminate key words in their searches like "young nude." Following is a post from their site. "At first, it doesn't make sense. When it comes to prostitution, human trafficking, and commercial sexual exploitation – men are the problem. That's the truth, plain and simple. Men are the traffickers, the pimps, the modern-day slave traders, the customers, the johns. In short, men are the bad guys. That's why we are gathering up a network of men who have had enough. As men, we are taking a stand against anyone who exploits women and girls. Now is the time to declare our strength and virtue; to use our unique abilities as men to help end this horrible crime. Yes, men are the problem. But together, we must be part of the solution." (End post) Makes you want to stand up and cheer, right?! (It looks like Menapat took their site down, but we are keeping this post, because it is such a great call to action.)

The men's groups that exist can consider taking on some action like Menapat (www.menapat.org) did and also incorporate as part of their program other actions that create a culture that supports loving relationships between men and women like "A Call to Men," (www.acalltomen.org) is doing. This group works to create a world where all men and boys are loving and respectful and all women and girls are valued and safe. You can listen to Tony Porter's "Ted" talk at this site. You will most likely be able to relate. Many men's groups are working to bring these issues up as part of their programming. If your men's group isn't addressing porn and how sexualized our culture has become, it is important that you start talking about it. We need a greater movement of men to work with each other to reduce domestic violence, porn, sex addiction and the fantasy of being with a prostitute.

Conclusion: For those of you who are counting, Chapter Three and Four offered over 50 ideas under 33 categories in a quick overview. The rest of the chapters have more actions with a lot more detail as you need to understand the dynamics and laws of an issue like porn if you are going to fight it. You are welcome to skim and then focus on the areas that interest you. For instance, if you feel called to protect the most vulnerable kids, like foster kids, then focus on that chapter and go to all the websites. If not, then skim through that chapter but do read it because while you may not be called to this aspect of the "supply" side of trafficking, you may meet someone who is and you can be an advocate. So read all of it, then choose that which you are the most passionate about and get to work! The purpose of this book is to facilitate you in finding where you are called to take action and empower you to do that.

References: (4.1) Common theme used by the Romeo Pimp as told by victims who do not want to be identified.

(4.2)The Register-Guard, "A Great Escape," 07.06.14 Josephine Woolington

(4.3) U-Tube video of Theresa Flores of www. traffickfree.org that was shown by Sister Bryant at St. Mary's Church 02.08.14

(4.4) KULR News "Truckers Raising Awareness About Human Trafficking" by Katie Chen, 6.14.14

(4.5) Truckers Against Trafficking website.

(4.6) Class on Domestic Violence at Cal State Fullerton.

(4.7) Interview with Sister Ines, SEA Charter Schools.

(4.8) MST project, Saddleback Human Trafficking Conference. 1.11.1

CHAPTER FIVE

Fair Trade and Labor Trafficking

We need to raise awareness as to the importance of purchasing "Fair Trade" products. In Third World countries, children are often used in agricultural industries like sugar and literally "worked to death." In these same countries, the Traffickers will often buy the oldest child from very poor families so the rest of the family can eat for a year. That child will then be locked in a brothel for the rest of their short life. In India, children as young as 9 months old are kept in cages, imprisoned in dark and inhuman conditions and sold for sex. *(5.1)* The Traffickers lie to the desperately poor parents who sell their children. Often, the parents think their children will be going to homes where they could have a better life or they are forced to sell their children to pay back loans.

You can react to this information in one of two ways. You can weep and then go out and talk about how terrible it all is and that will be the end of it. Or you can weep and then take action like doing awareness raising events regarding the importance of purchasing Fair Trade products that this chapter covers. You can also raise money to support Micro-Financing in Third World countries and use the suggestions in Chapter Eleven to do that. You can do your part to reduce child porn,

Many children who are victims of labor trafficking do not reach adulthood.

the fastest growing aspect of the porn industry by following the suggestions in Chapter Seven and Eight in order to reduce the demand for the sex trafficking of children. You can also support how important it is to educate people in Third World countries regarding Human Rights so that a shift occurs in their cultural values, so that it becomes more of a challenge to exploit the vulnerable. Low self-esteem makes women vulnerable to becoming trafficked.

We can encourage our government to focus more aid resources on specialized law enforcement and judicial training program that address human trafficking concerns. The International Justice Mission has shown the success of this effort. Their initiative reduced the availability of minors for sex trafficking by 79 percent in Cebu, and IJM has experienced similar successes in Cambodia. *(5.2)* We are only going to end this inhumane treatment of people through prayer and action.

Before you go any further into this chapter, take a minute to view Kevin Bales "Ted Talk." It will give meaning to the actions recommended in this chapter. Of the over 27 million Trafficking victims in the world, the ILO tells us that @2/3rds are labor trafficking victims and who is creating the demand for slave labor is YOU and ME. We can impact labor trafficking in the developing world by refusing to purchase any products produced by slaves. All you have to do is download the app at this site, www.free2work.org onto your phone. This app can scan the bar code of anything you want to buy and let you know if slave labor was used. If it was, then write to the company and let them know you won't buy their products until they are slave free.

One family used a similar app on their way home from a store and to their horror they found out that all the baby clothes they had just bought had been made by slaves in Brazil! *(5.3)* They took them back and within a year the company went off the list of companies who use slave labor. A new label will soon make its way onto clothing in the U.S. and Columbia. The "Freedom Seal" will certify that the article of clothing is "slave free." There is a concern that if there was no more slave labor, the cost of products will go up. In his book "Ending Slavery" Kevin Bales makes the point that starved slaves are not productive. Paid workers are far more productive. At a talk I attended, the speaker demonstrated that one company would only need to charge 32 more cents per Teddy Bear if they no longer used slave labor.

For the children making rugs or who are involved in other industries that are part of labor trafficking, they work 15 to 16 hours a day and often do not reach adulthood. *(5.4)* In his book "Ending Slavery," Kevin Bales tell the story of Raj, who was kidnapped at the age of eight and taken hundreds of miles away to another village where he was locked in a hut and forced to work from dawn to dusk, bent over a loom making rugs. He was fed very little and beaten if his work slacked off. We can do our part to end child labor in the rug trade by urging all our rug re-sellers to make sure that all the imported rugs they sell have the "Rug Mark" seal which certifies that the rug is "slave free."

There are some great groups who are raising awareness regarding labor abuses, like "Slave Free Seas" who is working to make people aware of slave labor at sea. The laborers in the fishing industry are made to work 20 hour days, are often kept in chains and sold. *(5.5)* There were enough protests outside Apple stores, that Apple listened and became the first electronics company to join the Fair Labor Association at the beginning of 2012. *(5.6)* This means that if you bought an Apple product before that, you may have been supporting human trafficking in the form of labor trafficking. Think of what you use that is electronic, like cell phones, computers, etc. It could have been made by slaves.

This is something people the developed countries do not understand and it is important that we raise awareness regarding that fact. It is a common assumption that we would not be letting products into our country if it was made by slave labor, but that is not how it works. While the thirteenth amendment forbids any business activity that supports slavery, it is not being enforced. We need to urge our government to enforce our laws and urge all companies that sell any product, including electronic products, to join the Fair Labor Association.

Enough people have written Hershey that they agreed to have 100% of their cocoa be Fair Trade by 2020. At the end of 2013, they reached a benchmark of 10%. *(5.7)* One of the points Kevin Bales made in his book "Ending Slavery," is that Chocolate companies like Mars, Nestle, Hershey, etc. are all in competition with each other, which makes it difficult for any one of them to go Fair Trade. They would all need to sit down at the same table and agree to only use Fair Trade chocolate. Senators Engle and Harkins did get all the chocolate companies to sit down at the same table and sign a protocol in 2001 that paved the way for a detailed plan to eliminate the use of slaves and child labor in the cocoa industry, however progress is slow. *(5.8)* While the corruption in Third World countries makes it difficult to purchase cocoa that is "slave free," we need to keep writing to this industry and tell them to "step up" their efforts to eliminate slave labor from their supply chains.

In a similar way we need to pressure the electronic, clothing and pig iron industries, etc. to get together and agree to stop using slaves and sign a pact and then announce their commitment to the public. There are individual companies that are doing this, but we need an entire industry to commit in order to move forward in a powerful way. Most companies have Fair Labor policies for their manufacturers and distributors and they do inspections to make sure they are complying.

However, the workers may be threatened to lie about the hours they are working and how would an inspector know that? Or the local inspector could be bribed to make a good report. Companies need to be very aggressive about enforcing their policies.

The following example demonstrates how Fair Trade protects people from becoming Trafficking victims. In the Nov/Dec 2006 newsletter of Green America, in their article entitled "Fair Trade Rice Makes Its Debut," Kyra tells her story of having worked with rice farmers in Thailand as part of the Educational Network for Global and Grassroots Exchange (ENGAGE), an organization that connects students who are studying abroad with projects in their host communities. Kyra shares how Fair Trade networks protect farmers from being cheated by the local mill operator for their products. Due to the corruption of the mill operators, the farmers will often wind up with three times more debt than their annual income. So they go to the cities for jobs and often wind up becoming Trafficking victims. While most food products like rice are locally grown, the aromatic brands like Jasmine do come from Asia. In addition to rice, TransFair USA also certifies coffee, tea, cocoa, chocolate, sugar, vanilla, bananas, mangoes, pineapples, and grapes.

Fair Trade means that no child or slave labor was used and that farmers receive a fair wage for their product and can afford to feed, educate and protect their children. We can help improve the living conditions of people in in the Third World so they can protect their families from becoming victims of Trafficking by asking our stores to make sure that all their food products that are imported are certified Fair Trade.

What is really encouraging is the number of companies that have taken a stand against slave labor like Whole Foods Market has done with their "Whole Trade" products. Not only does Whole Foods carry a lot of Fair Trade products like Chia seeds, spices and fruit, they have a line entitled "Whole Trade" meaning that Whole Foods is vouching that the farmers they partner with do not use slaves. This is important because many small famers cannot afford the Fair Trade certification for their products. We need more companies to help small, slave free farmers to get their products to market as "Fair Trade." In addition, for their

"Whole Trade" products, Whole Foods donates 1% of the sales to the Whole Planet Foundation who provides grants and loans to the self-employed poor.

The Fair Trade products that people use the most often include chocolate, coffee, tea, sugar, wine and clothing. 2.25 billion cups of coffee and 3.5 billion cups of tea are consumed in the world every day. If it all was Fair Trade, it would change the world completely! If the idea of disciplining yourself to only purchase Fair Trade is a little overwhelming, then start with coffee, tea and sugar as you use those items almost every day. Then again, while chocolate is a little pricey we need to consider all the African children who are working in the cocoa fields with bleeding feet and are beaten, before we choose the less expensive non-Fair Trade chocolate to buy. Dagoba Fair Trade, Organic Chocolate Powder sells at Amazon for $40 for 5 pounds. (50 cents an ounce)

"Wholesome Sweeteners," which is organic Fair Trade sugar, sells for $3.59 a pound or @$20 for a 10 pound bag at Amazon. Fair Trade coffee costs about the same as an upscale brand like Starbucks and given how many pesticides are sprayed on coffee and tea, it is well worth the $7.50 at Trader Joes and Target to buy organic, Fair Trade coffee. We need more major chains to create their own brands for Fair Trade products, like Trader Joes has done, to keep the price down. "Fair Trade USA" has a list of stores that carry Fair Trade products. As part of your awareness raising activities, you really want to make it your goal to have people use only Fair Trade coffee and tea because drinking these beverages is something they do every day. Every time they reach for the can of coffee or tea in the morning, they will be reminded of the fact that there are slaves in the world. In essence, you will have created a daily awareness campaign and who knows what that may lead to?!

In addition to being personally responsible for buying Fair Trade, there are many ways you can do your part to raise awareness. At the "Fair Trade Europe" website is a link under the "Activities" tab that supports one in participating in "World Fair Trade Day," which happens on the second Saturday of May. Many school fundraisers sell "World's Finest Chocolate" which *is* Fair Trade. You could promote that fact in the literature that gets sent home with the child as many people do not even know what "Fair Trade" means, so we need to start using opportunities like the school fundraiser to educate them.

Many churches sell chocolate for Easter. We need to urge them to only sell Fair Trade chocolate and at that table have a sign that reads "We do not sell any chocolate that was made by slaves." That should get a conversation going! Have a handout with a list of companies that do use slaves and a list that do not. Better yet, write to the companies that use slave labor and let them know that your church will no longer be selling their chocolate at Easter or any other event and that you are recommending this same action to every faith community in your area. That will get their attention!

If you belong to a singles group ask the leadership if you can put up a display table with Fair Trade Products and flyers educating people how Fair Trade prevents Human Trafficking. What groups do you belong to? What groups do your friends belong to? Ask them if you can invite a speaker to their group to talk about Fair Trade. What about your church's donut sales? Serve Fair Trade coffee and have a placard that promotes that next to the coffee. How about your annual church fair? You could host a table at the fair with Fair Trade products as the visual makes the idea of purchasing "Fair Trade" real for people. Include products from local stores. If you make it easy for people, they will take action. What would really get a conversation started is to put on your table products people use every day like spices, coffee, etc. and label the product with the grade that "Free 2 Work" has given the company. People will be intrigued and ask why one company got an "F" and another a "B." For those of you who are entrepreneurs, you can start a "Ten Thousand Villages" store. These stores make it possible for people to easily find a place where they can buy gifts that they feel good about.

There are other creative ways you could raise awareness. You could sell re-usable shopping bags that state: "Save children from Human Trafficking by purchasing Fair Trade products" to members of your service group. Have the youth sell them at your place of worship. As people shop they will raise awareness with the bags everywhere they go. The

Selling reusable bags that promote Fair Trade creates advocates.

average family uses 1200 plastic bags a year, so your effort would also go a long way towards protecting the environment and reduce Global Warming. The United Nations Environment Program estimated in 2006 that every square mile of ocean hosts 46,000 pieces of floating plastic. There is a garbage dump full of plastic in the North Pacific Ocean that is twice the size of the United States. *(5.9)*

While we are at it we can sell re-usable glass or metal water bottles that promote Fair Trade as according to the Clean Air Council, 2.5 million plastic bottles are trashed every hour in the U.S. In the U.K. over nine billion plastic bottles were trashed last year. The production of any plastic container puts toxins in the environment and consumes a lot of fossil fuels which accelerates Global Warming.

Many issues like Global Warming, impact people's vulnerability to becoming trafficked, because Global Warming is causing crops to die which impacts everyone, especially the poor. Global Warming is causing people to migrate, which makes families even more vulnerable to becoming Trafficking victims. In order to keep from starving, desperate families sell their children to the Traffickers. Of all the victim stories I have heard, the one that completely broke my heart was when I witnessed a young Asian teen weeping in the telling of how his older sister was sold to the Traffickers so he could eat. Chapter Fourteen addresses actions we can take to reduce Global Warming.

The website "Not for Sale" (www.notforsalecampaign.org) has a "Freedom Sunday" event the first Sunday of Lent, with materials they will send you to help you set up an awareness event regarding "Human Trafficking" where you could include activities like "Fair Trade" awareness that your group wants to promote. Just enter "Freedom Sunday" in their search bar. They also have a "Freedom Sabat" for the first day of Passover. These events get posted around the beginning of the year.

At the "Free2Work" site is a drop down menu under "Industry." You can select an industry like "herbs and spices" and you will find all your major brands. "Click" on their grade and then select "View Score Card." Next will be an overview on how well this company is working to prevent slave labor in their supply chains. Also on that page are specific reports on industries like the Electronic industry, Coffee industry and/or the Apparel industry, which are all major abusers of child and forced labor.

If you go through your house with the list, you might be surprised and shocked by the degree you are personally creating a demand for slave labor, given how many products you are using that employs slaves. I certainly was. This is a "wake up call" that everyone should engage in. Make it a party and go house to house with your friends. Drink some wine, look through each other's cupboards and then their closets for brand name clothes that use sweat shops to make their clothes. You could make this part of your Bunco parties or include it as part of your "Candle" or "Pots and Pans" parties that women do. Talk it up!

We need to encourage all of our stores and restaurants, especially coffee stores, to stock slave free products and promote what Fair Trade means so the public is willing to spend the extra money. Not only does purchasing Fair Trade products protect kids from Human Trafficking in the Third World, it also helps the economy in the developed world as businesses cannot compete with other businesses where the people who work there are not being paid.

You can find a complete report of what products are used by slave or child labor by going to the U.S Department of Labor website, www.dol.gov and in their search bar at the top right, type in "2013" (2014) List of Goods Produced by Child Labor or Forced Labor." We have the ability to change the world with our buying power. If we refused to purchase products produced by slave labor then there would be no market for the slave traders. Companies would respond to public demand for "slave free" products by promoting at their website that they have been responsible for not using child or slave labor in the manufacturing and distribution of their products. If everyone did their part, then millions of children would no longer be robbed of their childhood.

The California Attorney General's office is working to educate the business community on how to monitor their supply chains. We can encourage businesses to contact the Attorney General's office for more information. Every state can pass an act similar to the" California Transparency Act" which is designed to eliminate slave labor from supply chains. For those of you who live in California, you can Google this and learn how to use this act to hold California companies responsible and use social media to raise awareness regarding this act. Verite.org explains this act in laymen's terms. Just search for "California" to find the Transparency Act.

The "California Transparency Act" refers to manufacturing and distribution companies that are based in California. What about retailers? In Europe they have many "Fair Trade Towns." The idea is catching on in the U.S. What this means is that city councils pass ordinances that require retail stores to make sure that none of the products they sell are produced by slaves. This link provides the plan to make a "Fair Trade Town" happen. http://fairtradecampaigns.org/campaign-type/towns/

There is a great phone app entitled "Slavery Footprint." It comes with a survey that lets you know how many slaves were used to support your current lifestyle which is a great personal wake up call. Users of the app can send a message to a company to learn about its position on forced labor. It includes a "check-in" feature on Facebook to let stores know about your interest in "slave free" products. This group also has the survey at their website. You enter your zip code, age, number of children, how many electronic devices you use and how many items of clothes you have. My survey let me know that 44 slaves work for me! Yikes!!! That is disturbing. What I love about this survey is that it brings the issue "home" for people. If you have a captive audience like a youth group, you could have them pull out their cell phones when you meet and take the survey. It would make for a great discussion afterwards. "Slavery Blueprint" also has a platform for companies with a blueprint to help them identify high-risk areas for trafficking suppliers.

Have your group take on the worst offenders and write to them. If that company is not responsive, then you can move to the next step. At your awareness raising event you could have petitions that people sign that you can send to the worse abusers. Many stay at home moms ask me what they can do. You can pass around a petition while you are at your child's soccer game or bring one to your MOPS (Mothers of Pre-Schoolers) group.

All you need to do is put at the top of the page: "Dear (name of organization), It has come to our attention that many of your products are produced with slave labor. (Let them know in your letter the grade "Free to Work" has given them.) Given our commitment to end Human Trafficking, (name of faith community, organization etc.) is raising awareness as to who to purchase from and who to boycott. Please do what you can to eliminate child and slave labor from all your supply chains and the production and distribution of your product." Have people sign and send to the president of that organization. All you have to do is Google "Who is the president of (name of company)" to find that out. It doesn't work to use the "contact us" option at a company website, because that email will just go to someone in customer service. A "snail mail" letter is what you need to send in order to be heard.

Kevin Bales suggests that we take actions like making sure the investment of our mutual funds and retirement accounts are screened to exclude any profit from slavery. Our reluctance to take the time to be socially responsible for how we purchase and to write to companies demanding slave free products is creating a market for labor trafficking. If enough Faith groups and community organizations took this on, I promise you companies will change their policies and together we can end labor trafficking.

References: (5.1) Independent IE, (Ireland) "Irish 'buy' Indian children to save them from brothels." Niamh Horan – 20 October 2013
(5.2) The Daily Signal. "How Asia, U.S. Can Help End Human Trafficking." 03.21.15 Olivia Enos
(5.3) Presentation by Sister Mary Bryant, St. Mary's church, 3.08.14
(5.4) Stephen Bauman, Vanguard 2014 conference, "Why is she a Slave?"
(5.5) Maritime Executive, "Fishing Slaves Off New Zealand" 06.04.14 Wendy Laursen.
(5.6) Post at "The Fair Labor Association" site. January 2012
(5.7) Global Exchange - Hershey's and Fair Trade: Is it a Victory? 7th May, 2013 - Posted by Zarah Patriana
(5.8) "Ending Slavery, How We Free Today's Slaves" by Kevin Bale
(5.9) Courier Mail.com AU, Floating Rubbish Dump in the Pacific Ocean, bigger than the U.S. Xavier La Canna AAP, February 03, 2008

CHAPTER SIX

Protect the Most Likely Victim From the Trafficker- the 5 Prong Plan

In addition to raising awareness, we need to protect the most likely victims from being trafficked which are street kids, foster kids and immigrants. According to "Stand Up for Kids," a third of the kids on the street in the U.S are under 15. www.Childrensrights.org tell us that as many as 30% of kids who age out of the foster care system struggle with homelessness. The rest of the kids on the street are kids who ran away from abuse or their families are homeless, etc. A U.S. Department of Health and Human Services study found that 46% of homeless youth left their home because of physical abuse, 17% left because of sexual abuse. Once a kid hits the streets, within 48 hours 1 out of 3 will be approached by a Human Trafficker. Once that kid is picked up they will be dead in 3 to 7 years from Aids, suicide, getting beaten to death, etc. By reducing the number of street kids and protecting immigrants, we make it harder to be in the business of Human Trafficking for every country in the world.

Within 48 hours of a kid hitting the streets, 1 out of 3 will be solicited.

We protect kids by keeping them from hitting the streets and rescuing those who are on the street. There is one church in the U.S. for every 3 kids on the street, yet 13 kids a day die on our streets. There is one faith community in the U.S. for each and every child in the foster care systems, yet only 25% of those who are adoptable ever get adopted and there are never enough foster parents. *(6.1)* For the most part, we have these statistics because these kids are "invisible."

If we had a ministry at every church, synagogue, mosque, temple, parent group, etc. that got their community involved in taking care of vulnerable kids, as an aligned faith community we could significantly reduce the number of kids who live a life of unbearable desperation. Once people start getting involved with these kids in some way like a mentor, etc., they often take on more and more as they come to understand the need. It is not enough to have a speaker come once a year or every two years to a church or organization to talk about foster care, adoption or mentoring. You need an activity at least twice a year, every year.

We need a driving force at our places of worship to take on these kids. We can act to protect the most likely victim by raising awareness for and encouraging volunteering for those organizations that support 1. Adoption and Foster care. 2. Mentoring. 3. Runaway Prevention. 4. Protecting the Immigrant. 5. Rescue and Shelter for Homeless Teens. If everyone spent two hours a week volunteering to help somewhere, we could transform our nation and the world regarding the future of kids. At the very least, even if one is not available to be a mentor etc., we can all attend orientations to find out what is involved and be an advocate for foster parenting, mentoring, etc.

Foster Care and Adoption

Before the 1940's, in the U.S. churches ran the orphanages and we had a ministry at almost every church to encourage people to adopt. Because the orphanages were connected to the church, pastors promoted taking on these kids. When the state took over, we lost our ownership of the "orphan." In most developed countries, there is a program similar to the foster care system that is in the U.S. with the same perception, which is that foster kids are the government's responsibility and as a faith community we will "help out." That position is not working.

As a faith community, we need to either birth or recover our commitment to the "orphan." We need to take a stand that every child will have a healthy family to be part of and that it is our job, not the government's job to make sure these children are taken care of. There are several organizations that work with faith communities that have taken this stand so we already have working models that we will review in this chapter. The foster care system is overwhelmed in every country in the world. We need to step up our efforts to make the needs of these kids known as these vulnerable kids and homeless kids are the most likely group to become trafficking victims.

My definition of an "orphan" is a kid who is not connected to a family which could include a baby in the womb that the mother does not want or a kid in the foster care system or a kid who is a runaway and does not want to go back to their biological family because their mother is a drug addict who wants to pimp them out or a kid who has no family because their parents died. Many people share my definition and have expanded their mission for their "Respect Life" ministries to include foster and street kids. Christian Centers that are providing pregnancy tests and counseling women to keep their babies see homeless youth all the time. They really support this type of "ministry," because everyone needs to be part of a family. A pregnant, homeless girl with no family support is at great risk for herself and her baby becoming exploited.

Places of worship can ask a speaker to come from a local foster care organization to speak after all the services and host a table outside to answer questions. In my experience, if you invite people to come to a meeting, very few come. However if you give a speaker 3 minutes to talk at the end of the service many people will come out to get information. Sometimes they are looking for information for a friend or family member who has been thinking of foster care or adoption.

Faith Communities can host a "Heart Gallery" Sunday. The Heart Gallery will bring displays of kids who are looking for "forever families." The displays have the child's photo and a short description sharing their dreams for their life. In the third chapter, on the page before the section entitled "Be A Community Activist" is a picture of a "Heart Gallery" display at a mall. This program is very impactful. You can go to their website www.heartgalleryofamerica.org for more information. You can also Google "Heart Gallery" with your U.S. County in the search.

Your local state foster care agency should have the number for the local rep for "The Heart gallery." If your country does not have a similar program, you could get some photographers together and start a program. The Heart Gallery website has tips on how to do that and it would be a worthwhile effort as foster care agencies will tell you this program is the most effective they have seen to recruit adoptive parents of older kids. Any activity that your group does that "puts a face" to these kids makes them real, which creates compassion and participation.

What many people are unaware of is that foster kids in group homes cannot go anywhere without an adult who has been "vetted" by the system. They can't go to a friend's house after school or to a party or to the mall with their friends. As a consequence for bad behavior we "ground" our own kids from social activities. Foster kids in group homes are permanently "grounded" not because of their bad behavior, but because of the behavior of their parents. Many churches have responded to the lack of social activities available to kids in group homes by creating activities at their churches like a Pumpkin Carving event for Halloween or a picnic where the kids can come and play basketball or touch football and eat. The best kind of project is one where it is done every month with the majority of the volunteers being the same people, so the kids get to know them and feel safe to open up. Anytime you can provide the sense for these kids that they are part of a community, it gives them hope.

For those of you who want to be an advocate for these kids, attend an orientation to find out what is involved in becoming a foster or adoptive parent. At that meeting, you will meet adoptive and foster parents who have made it all work. By sharing their "success stories" you will motivate people to take these children in, as people have concerns about parenting these kids. The greatest need is for people to adopt sibling sets and teens. I shared this with an infertile couple who always wanted a big family and liked the idea of taking in kids who were related.

I met a woman who took in a 17 year old as a foster parent and offered to adopt the girl. The young girl asked her why she was bothering to do that as she would be 18 in a few months. The foster mother answered... "While that may be true, a mother is forever!" That statement completely transformed that young girl's life as that statement validated that she finally had that which she had always wanted, a "forever" family. You and I can't even begin to comprehend what is it like to feel like you do not belong to any family and then to be provided with a sense that you do belong to someone. There is even a form of adoption for kids over 18, so they can feel truly accepted and part of a family.

Foster care is truly an unselfish calling and one that is very rewarding for those who are called to this type of ministry and it truly is a ministry. While there is a real need for adoptive parents, there is an even greater need for good foster parents. The foster parent is the ultimate mentor and even if the kids go back to families with less than desirable circumstances where there is abuse, just not enough to justify them being in the system, these kids always remember the care they got from their foster parents. They will model that with their own children. It transforms a person's world view to be exposed to another way to live life. Otherwise they will revert to the only way they know.

Focus on the Family did a survey of what how the public viewed kids in foster care. They shared the results of their survey at a meeting for church leaders on promoting adoption. The two top assumptions were that kids were in the foster care system because they were troubled kids who were in and out of the juvenile justice system and that it is very expensive to adopt. The fact is that kids are in the foster care system almost exclusively because of who their parents are, not because of what they did.

My foster son cried himself to sleep for over a year, grieving the loss and rejection of his birth parents. He would mumble over and over again "if only I was cuter or smarter or funnier," then wail in anguish because he truly thought he wasn't good enough for a mother or father to want him. It was heart breaking. Through counseling and my unwavering validation of him, he finally accepted that it was his drug addicted birth parents who had the problem, not him. Once he got that, he really began to blossom.

When I took him in at the age of 6, he used the "F" word a lot because that is what he heard. When I explained to him that other parents would not want him playing with their kids if he used that word, he stopped. Yes, the older kids have bad habits but kids are resilient and they want it to work. However, they will test you. My son used to call me an "old, fat cow." He did that because he needed to know if I would keep him no matter how bad his behavior, before he would open up his heart to me. These kids think they must have done something really bad to have their parents reject them, except they can't figure out what it was, so they are hypersensitive to being rejected. Once he was done testing me, he stopped with the insults and made an effort to bond with me. It is important that foster and adoptive parents understand the "testing" phase and utilize the counseling services the state provides so the necessary and important bonding process happens with these kids.

What motivates me to do what I do is the thought of a child like my foster/adoptive son who will go through so much loss, pain and loneliness, who never gets adopted or with a good foster family and winds up a victim of Human Trafficking. My adopted son brought this issue "home" for me. What about this issue brings it "home" for you?

With regard to the costs, if one adopts a child from the foster care system in the U.S., it costs a few hundred dollars to adopt which you will get back as a tax credit. One infertile woman told me that she really wanted more children and had thought of adoption but she couldn't afford the $40,000 it cost to adopt. Once I explained the true costs of adopting through the state, within a couple of weeks she and her husband went to an orientation to find out more. In most states, even after you adopt you will continue to receive the same monthly stipend that you received as a foster parent so you can afford to put your child in sports, etc. Also all their dental, medical and counseling is paid for and you can include your biological children in the counseling to help your own children adjust. Different states have different benefits, so you will need to confirm what your state offers.

When children come into the systems that are Mexican, Vietnamese, etc., not only do they lose their family, they lose their culture. There is a real need for Foster/Adoptive parents that are Spanish speaking, Vietnamese and other distinct cultural groups. In Orange County, California about half the population is Spanish speaking, mostly Mexican, yet a CASA staff member shared with me that only 17% of CASA's are Spanish speaking. (6.2) I have heard various opinions as to why this so, but the one that makes the most sense is that in their countries of origin the concept of mentoring or foster care does not exist. They are unfamiliar with the process because in countries like Mexico and Vietnam, there are only orphanages. So go to an orientation for foster/adoption and mentoring and look for opportunities to speak and promote the need into those communities that are underrepresented.

Once people take these kids into their homes, they need support from the community. A meeting once a month at your place of worship, where foster parents can share their challenges and get support can often mean the difference between success and failure for that placement. Offering to "Kid Sit" for a foster family is a real gift for that family and may be the perfect way for you to contribute your special gifts to this whole effort to ensure that every child has a healthy family to be part of.

KidSave is another great program where a family can host a kid from the foster care system or from overseas for a weekend or a few weeks. The KidSave program results in a lot of adoptions, because once a family has had an opportunity to live with a foster kid, all their erroneous perceptions about these kids are put aside and they fall in love with the kids. If the host family or single individual is not in a position to adopt the child, they act as advocates for the child by promoting what a great kid they are sponsoring to their sphere of influence. They ask their friends and associates to help them find an adoptive family and are often successful in doing that.

The other side of this issue is that it costs the state a fortune to keep a child in foster care and for that reason, states have to make cuts in their programs all the time and who loses are vulnerable kids. By adopting the kids who are available for adoption we make more room in the system for kids who should be in the system. By addressing root causes and doing our part to reduce child abuse, poverty, teen pregnancy, etc. we reduce the number of kids who need to go into the foster care system.

The Traffickers target kids coming out of orphanages in those countries with an orphanage system. Some countries turn the kids out into the streets at the age of 16. The care these children receive will make you weep. They often receive very little attention and if they need a tooth pulled, it is often without Novocain as there is no money for these kids for anything. For those of you who feel called to adopt children abroad, agencies who specialize in this can provide information regarding tax credits, etc. However, some of these agencies are corrupt, so be careful. You can raise awareness to the plight of international orphans by including mission trips to orphanages in the Third World, as part of your faith outreach.

Mentoring

In interviewing with all the different organizations that fight Trafficking and protect kids, mentoring came up over and over again as the activity that made the greatest difference for the least amount of effort, that protect kids from becoming victims. The Traffickers target any kid without strong family support like kids in group homes. Mentoring entails a commitment of about 6 to 8 hours a month and positively impacts the way a kid views his/her world and his/her future. Foster kids know that staff is paid to help them. The fact that you care enough to spend time with a kid without getting paid, especially for a kid whose life experience is that "no one cares," can completely "rock that kid's world," and provide hope where there was no hope for a better future. They will model their mentor because they want to be like him/her. Mentoring offers a kid the opportunity to experience a world that can be very different from the only one they have known.

If the only environment a kid has been exposed to is a gang community, being with someone who knows how to succeed in the world legally can start that kid thinking in a different way. Many people are intimidated by the idea of being a friend to a troubled kid. It does take some skill which is why mentoring organizations offer training because many of these kids have had their trust betrayed and they won't open up to you without giving you some kind of test to make sure you won't reject them. In other words, some are going to be obnoxious.

They "test" to see if you will reject them by doing the things you don't like, so if you don't like the "'F'" word they will use it. *(6.3)* One gentleman shared about picking up a kid who was from a gang community, to take him on an outing. As soon as the teen got in the car the teen said, "Nice car, I would love to steal myself one of these!" To which the gentleman calmly responded… "You could do that or I could teach you how to earn one." The teen got very quiet for a long minute. Then he looked up and said…"You would do that, for me?!" No one had ever gone out of their way for that kid before. It might take a while for these kids to accept that you genuinely care, that you aren't going to try to take advantage of them in some way.

CASA, which stands for "Court Appointed Special Advocate," is a great program in the U.S. for Faith Communities and parent groups to promote. (www.casaforchildren.org) A CASA is empowered to be an advocate, to make recommendations to the court and foster care system regarding the child's welfare. What this means is that in addition to being a mentor, they write reports that the judge considers regarding the child's welfare. One CASA who had been assigned to a 10 year old boy who wasn't doing well in school, shared with me that she took him for a walk so he could relax and feel safe to talk. Then she asked him why he thought he wasn't doing well in school and he said "I can't see." So the CASA petitioned the child welfare system to get him glasses. His grades immediately improved.

That story often elicits outrage from people because they don't realize how overburdened our social workers and foster parents are. A social worker in Los Angeles could have as many as 30 children or more that they are responsible for. In addition, these kids often don't communicate what they need. They have given up on anyone really caring

Mentoring can prevent child exploitation.

what happens to them which only underlines how important it is to get involved. We can either stand on the sidelines and be critical of the government's efforts or the efforts of organizations that are working to help these kids, or we can take ownership and make sure these kids have a family that will be there for them.

Judges know that having a mentor is one of the most effective ways to protect kids and get their life on the right track, so many Traffic Courts are showing a short video on what it means to be a CASA (Court Appointed Special Advocate) while people are waiting for Traffic school. This is something all Traffic School programs could be doing. So recommend it to your local court and then set up a table at the lunch break and answer questions and invite people to schedule themselves for a CASA orientation. (www.casaforchildren.org) This is one way to be a powerful advocate for an organization to protect kids from becoming victims.

CASA has a fabulous program entitled "Family Connections." Social workers are so overworked that they simply don't have the time to keep calling back if people don't return their calls or if they can't immediately find a family member for a child. "Family Connections" is headed up by one paid staff member and a group of volunteers who will do the intensive work needed to try and find at least one healthy family member for the child to be placed with as there tends to be more stability with blood relatives. *(6.4)*

Charlotte, (not her real name) was referred to this program by her CASA. Charlotte's was failing in school and given her lack of stability at home, Charlotte's CASA was concerned that Charlotte would be vulnerable to becoming a victim of Human Trafficking, once she "aged out" of the system. So "Family Connections" tried to find her father, a man Charlotte had never known in the hopes that he might be healthy enough and care enough, to be there for his daughter. Ten years ago when Charlotte first came into the system, her father had been found but because of his criminal activities, he would not have been a suitable parent and social services would not have allowed him to be responsible for a child.

At that time the father was told that there was a family who wanted to adopt his daughter so the father "gave it to God" and let his daughter go. However the adoption fell through and the father who was "out of the picture" at that time, did not know that. "Family Connections" found him and the man had gotten his life together. He was a pastor at a church and was married with two kids. The reunion was healing for both Charlotte and her father. Charlotte now lives with her father and is going to college and has a family and lots of relatives that she can now call her own.

In another instance, Steve, (not his real name) was suffering from severe depression and told his CASA that he was depressed because "he did not have anyone in the world who was family that he was connected to, who cared about him." He would be aging out of the system soon and as the days passed he grew more and more anxious about a future where he would be all alone. So "Family Connections" searched his records and found a distant aunt who Social Services had not been successful at being able to get a hold of.

"Family Connections" found the aunt and the story she told is a common one. Steve's father had been the "black sheep" of the family and had not spoken to his parents or any other family member for years. No one knew he had a son. The aunt told CASA that she would love to meet Steve and a meeting was set up at a park in the near future. Steve arrived and expected to meet three people, his aunt and a couple of her family members. About 40 people showed up and all assured Steve that he had a family that he was welcome to be part of. That experience completely and totally transformed Steve's entire world view of what his future would look like and what was possible for him. He began to do well in school. His depression became a thing of the past. Unfortunately, because of budget cuts CASA has had to cut this program in many locations. This is where you could ask your company to consider sponsoring the one staff member needed for a program like this. There are other opportunities like this one, where a company can sponsor a badly needed staff member for an organization.

The Mentor Federation (www.mentorfoundation.org) operates in

Arabia, Colombia, Germany, Latvia, Lithuania, Sweden, the UK and the USA. Big Brothers and Big Sisters is another great mentoring organization to promote in the U.S. The kids in the foster care system will go from their parents to a foster home, back to their parents, then another foster home, then a group home, etc. They are often changing families, social workers, etc. If a mentor is willing to commit to that child for years, they are often the only constant in that kid's life and any type of stability is important to the developmental stages of any child.

While attending a meeting sponsored by the Orange County Human Trafficking Task Force, a judge spoke about the difference an adult can have in a kid's life. He shared about a kid named James who was in and out of his courtroom on a regular basis until the janitor at James' school took an interest in James and befriended him. That friendship transformed that kid's life and the last time James was in court the judge acknowledged him for having stayed out of trouble. Then James shared with the judge his commitment to have a life that worked and how the janitor had inspired that commitment. The judge shared with the group at the OCHTTF meeting that his peers have witnessed over and over again that what makes the greatest difference in the life of a troubled kid is a mentor. A vulnerable kid's greatest defense against being lured by a Trafficker is to have a mentor, someone who will be there for them. You could and should ask your pastor if you could permanently keep a poster on the bulletin board where you worship, to promote the local mentoring organization.

In talking to many people about how impactful mentoring can be, I have run into several single mothers who were concerned about who may mentor their child. While all mentors have to be vetted by the FBI, that only tells one that the prospective mentor did not commit a crime. With a husband, you have influence. With a mentor one doesn't know what values that person has. Mothers of boys wonder....... "when their son asks the adult guy how to "get" girls, are they going to tell them to buy a condom and go for it?" Mentoring is so valuable to a child that these concerns should not stop one from seeking a mentor as you are not "locked in" to who you are matched with and can always talk to the mentor about your values. Most mentors feel that it is their job to support the parent-child relationship and will be receptive to what you need.

That being said, there is a need for Faith Groups to establish their own mentoring programs so Baptists can find a Baptist mentor for their child or a Catholic, etc. can find a Catholic mentor for their child as statistically if there is a man in a boy's life that they admire, they are three times more likely to continue going to church as an adult than if they only just see their mother going to church. The central organization of the church like a diocese can administer the program and require additional "vetting" like a letter from their pastor.

Mentors are truly the greatest people in the world and the rewards to a kid far exceed any risks. Mentoring organizations like Big Brothers and Big Sisters go to extra-ordinary lengths to make sure children are safe. In addition to fingerprinting and checking the FBI data base, a thorough in-person interview is conducted that explores a prospective mentor's childhood, past relationships, current family situation, how they spend their free time, recent and current employment, past experience with youth - volunteering or working, preferences for a mentee and more.

References include two friends over 1 year (non-related), employment and any past volunteer positions over the past 7 years. Once a match is established, every month the Match Support Specialist makes contact with the Caregiver, the Mentor and the Child. The Specialist makes sure all sides report the same outings/activities, no "grooming" or inappropriate physical contact, gift giving, etc. is taking place or beginning. (6.5)

The staff has ongoing training from professionals to recognize red flags. There are set policies such as no visits to the Volunteer's home for the first 6 months. Then it is up to the Caregiver and Match Support Specialist to approve. There are additional rules like "No overnight visits for the first 12 months." I bring all of this up because of the concern about pedophiles volunteering for a mentoring organization. Pedophiles don't want to be caught and all these checks would make a child predator nervous.

There are informal ways to be a mentor like an "after school" program, similar to what the janitor did for James. "Kid Care America" (www.kidcareamerica.org) helps Faith Communities start and sustain after school programs. This is an outstanding way for churches to get involved. You can identify kids at risk, become their friend and offer to support them by tutoring etc. Kids will never forget the generosity of another human being and you may be one of the few positive influences they have to help them make good choices. It will take an all community effort to protect the most vulnerable kids from becoming victims.

Runaway Prevention

For any awareness raising event that you do that addresses the needs of these kids, you can include flyers with volunteer information for the local runaway hotline. You could get a group to put up posters at transportation centers with the Runaway Hotline number. When runaways first hit a new town, they would not consider themselves to be a Trafficking victim and may not respond to the poster with the 888 number for Human Trafficking. You can partner with schools and ask them to raise awareness regarding the dangers of running away. The most effective presentations for kids take the form of a skit and a testimonial from a former runaway. "Stand up for Kids" and other organizations like it, have clients who are former runaways who will speak. You need to include information regarding what resources are available to kids who find themselves in an abusive situation as that often is why they are considering running away.

What I would love to see is groups of seniors at bus stations and train stations making themselves visible talking to runaways, so that the Traffickers no longer feel comfortable being there to find them. Let's run the Traffickers out of our transportation centers! Sometimes a runaway is a kid with a good family who had a fight with their parents and is trying to show their parent who is boss by running away. By the time they have hit their destination they have cooled down, but need encour-

agement to call their parents. Other times they are trying to escape abusive situations and need to be connected to a counselor. We need volunteers where the runaways are to help them find their way. Runaway
prevention is a powerful prevention strategy that should be part of any
campaign to reduce Trafficking.

Protecting the Immigrant

After street kids and foster kids, the third most vulnerable group to
becoming "trafficked" are immigrants. Of the over 2,000 foreign victims
that the "Amistad" movement served, 72% were trafficked for labor.
44% of that group were males. The "Amistad" movement is working to
help immigrant communities identify victims and provides help for rescued victims. For the legal, domestic immigrants the Traffickers will
often take kids and threaten to turn their parents, who are here illegally,
over to the U.S. Immigration and Customs Enforcement (ICE) if they
don't do everything they tell them to do. Pastors and other community
leaders need to meet with Homeland Security Investigations (HSI), the
investigative arm of the Department of Homeland Security. HSI will
reassure them that if anyone is threatened, they will take steps to protect
the family and HSI is separate from ICE. HSI needs the cooperation of
the community so they can catch the Traffickers. An Illegal immigrant's
fear of law enforcement is making the job of HSI very difficult because
the Traffickers are getting away with exploiting immigrants. As a result,
Human Trafficking is growing in immigrant communities.

This is where Faith Communities can help because immigrants in
faith communities will often try to get help from their church, synagogue, etc. A Pastor/Rabbi who has taken the time to meet with law
enforcement to find out how to protect victims and assure them that
they won't be deported if they come forward, becomes an asset to the
people in their faith community and to law enforcement. Often pastors
will turn victims over to an NGO who may not call in law enforcement
because of the fear of what might happen to the family of the victim.
Then the trafficker just victimizes another person which only encour-

ages them to keep victimizing immigrants in that community. If faith communities form a cooperative to protect victims and empower law enforcement to prosecute Traffickers, then the Traffickers will be taken off the streets and leave those communities alone. *(6.6)*

It is the job of HSI to investigate criminal organizations involved in cross-border crime. That includes the smuggling of drugs, weapons and counterfeit goods; human smuggling and trafficking; child pornography and exploitation; etc. People are confused because Homeland Security has both an investigative branch that addresses the smuggling of people and a branch that deals with illegal immigrants. However, think about it. If you report a crime, the police do not ask you for your immigration status when they come to make the report. It is not a question the investigative arm of Homeland Security will ask, nor are they required to report to the immigration branch of Homeland security if they find out someone is here illegally.

That being said, if someone is a victim of a qualifying crime and is cooperating with an investigation and is here illegally, HSI can provide them immediate legal status. Potentially, they can obtain a U or T-Visa and eventually become lawful permanent residents and United States citizens. HSI can also relocate victims, witnesses and family members if they have been threatened. This is important to know because victims are often told that their families will be hurt or killed if they do not do everything they are told. *(6.6)*

Many groups feel that in order to protect immigrants from being exploited, we need Immigration Reform. While a divisive issue, illegal immigrants and their children are vulnerable to all kinds of abuse from many types of criminals. There won't be any suggestions in this book for how to accomplish immigrant reform, because it is outside the scope of this book, but it is worth mentioning given how vulnerable immigrants are to becoming Trafficking victims.

Rescue and Shelter

Churches can also partner with "Safe Families" and their program.

(www.safe-families.org) This program is designed to keep kids out of the foster care system who don't belong there and to provide "safe environments for children." "Safe Families" acts as a bridge for a family in need with a family that can help the family in need. Both the kids and the families who take in kids are vetted so everyone feels "safe." The program matches a person with needs such as mentoring, temporary shelter, etc. to a member of a church who is willing to provide that need. For example, the program might support a single mother who has nowhere to leave her children while she looks for a job.

One of the Safe Families staff members shared with me the story of a single mother who grew up in the foster care system who had no extended family, absolutely no one to help her. She was about to lose her job because given the time she had to drop her two kids off at school, she was late to work almost every day. Now if that woman had lost her job and then her apartment and was living in her car, her children would have gone into the foster care system. These single mothers who are struggling just to get by, have a hard time getting their kids back, once they lose them. They often go into depression and may start drinking, etc. which could result in them losing their kids completely and then more kids wind up on the street. If one gets too overwhelmed by life, they just go numb.

Safe Families, through their church and community partnerships, found someone to take the mother's kids to school so she could keep her job. It was a really simple solution that saved three people from a life of heartache. This program also screens kids over 18 who temporarily need a place to stay. These kids will stay until they get a job or get their student loan in place, which is very difficult if one is homeless. This program should be part of every faith community in some form.

There are many people who would be willing to take in an 18 year old foster child who is "aging out" of the system, if they knew how to do that. We need more organizations like "Safe Families" who will assist in that and help people take in street kids, like Sandra Bullock's character did in the true story movie "The Blind Side." However, they need to feel "safe" to do that. Churches can partner with organizations that help street kids get their birth certificate, so we know who they are, where they have come from, if they committed a violent crime, etc. so we know if they are "safe" to live in someone's home or in a church-run house. At the very least, volunteers from faith communities can help organizations that take care of homeless kids, help the kids get their GED, their driver's license, or get to a job interview, etc.

In addition to keeping kids from becoming homeless, we also need to rescue those who have hit the streets. We do that by supporting those organizations that are actively involved in saving kids from the streets, like Stand up for Kids, Covenant House, etc. These organizations go out to the street to find homeless kids before the Traffickers do. These desperate kids are looking for a job in order to survive, so that is what the Traffickers offer them, jobs. These poor kids think their prayers have been answered. It is so cruel to take advantage of vulnerable kids like this.

In this section, we are referring to street outreach for homeless kids. In Chapter Thirteen, there is information on street outreach to people

Covenant House has 22 houses in the U.S., Canada and Latin America where a kid can stay until they are able to live on their own.

in the commercial sex industry and street prostitutes, which is a very different street outreach effort than what organizations like "Stand Up for Kids" and "Covenant House" are doing. "Stand up for Kids," which was founded in 1990, is all volunteer run and can train concerned citizens to go out to the streets to find homeless kids and what to do when you find them and how to be safe.

The kids at Covenant House learn life skills such as cooking and budgeting. They receive counseling, medical care, help getting their GED, putting together a resume and interviewing skills; all the things a parent provides. At Covenant House Los Angeles, 90% of the kids who complete their 1 to 2 year program are no longer homeless. Their success rate is high because they have a facility where they can provide stability, a "family" atmosphere and a comprehensive program. Any successful "rescue" attempt is going to need a permanent shelter and a program for the kids that builds confidence and life skills.

I had the opportunity to go out in the Covenant House outreach van. The homeless kids I met were the nicest, most polite group of kids I had ever met. Without exception there was real fear in their eyes, fear of the streets, fear of what might happen to them there. As a result of the "survival sex" many feel forced to engage in, a small percent of homeless kids suffer from AIDS. Being sick and on the streets is brutal.

What organizations like "Stand up for Kids" will tell you is that once they rescue kids, there is almost no shelter for them. In the rest of this section are suggestions for how churches could do their part to provide shelter. Large churches, such as mega-churches have the infrastructure and money to provide a facility for young prostitutes to come off the street. These churches will need to choose if they are going to take care of minors or people 18 or older, like Covenant House does.

Since 1979, "Children of the Night" has been successfully providing rehabilitation for former prostitutes who are minors and provides training on how to set this up as well as information regarding costs. "Children of the Night" has a lock down facility for kids 11 to 17 that has been set up like a home. The kids can come and go. The purpose of the lock down is to keep unwanted people out, as these kids need to feel safe from a former pimp who may be looking for them. The kids are allowed to have pets and become a family. They go to school at the facility and progress at their own rate. Given that they were former prostitutes, they have special needs and it works to put them together in a facility that addresses those needs.

Regenis Rising is a church model that takes in kids from the foster care system when they age out, before they hit the street. What is unique about the Regenisis Rising model is that it is built upon establishing individual and community connections for kids, something we take for granted. A homeless kid rarely has an adult they can talk to if they are feeling discouraged about life or an adult they can share their wins or children with.

With the Regenis Rising program, the kids have a life coach, a budget coach, pastoral support, professional counselors, volunteer "grandparents" who they have dinner with, who become the family that they can spend the holidays with. The volunteers and coaches help these kids get their GED, a job, finish school, etc. The Regenisis program is somewhat costly as they use paid staff, but it can be tweaked. There are churches that are using similar models with all volunteer help, including volunteer counselors and their costs are @$10,000 a year. You could partner with a college and provide internships for college kids who are working toward a Social Service or Psychology degree as a way to recruit high caliber volunteer help. Everyone asks me how these churches can do it for so little. The answer is that the kids are charged rent and the homes are donated.

Gone are the days when we left an emancipated teen at the courthouse. If the kids have no family they are taken to Transitional Living Shelters, but those shelters are all temporary and going from Transitional Shelter to Transitional Shelter is no life for a kid. The Traffickers hang out around these shelters looking for vulnerable kids. We need corporations, banks that have REO's, investors, etc. to consider donating homes to churches or other groups that want to take on sheltering kids. Apartment owners can donate a few apartments for transitional housing to organizations like Covenant House. There are grants to support "shelter" type programs but given that the biggest expense is the house, if that could be donated then faith communities would only need to do a few fundraisers to make it work.

We will always need institutional models like Covenant House for the kids who have been on the street and brutalized. Experts need to work with those kids and for that reason we need to support those organizations financially that offer this kind of help. Half of all the kids who have been picked up by Covenant House have experienced some sort of violence. They have been knifed, raped, beaten, etc. However, with the right intervention they do heal and would do well in a church-run program, once they have been through the type of program that Covenant House offers.

The ideal scenario would be for Faith Communities to partner with organizations that take care of street kids or former prostitutes, so once a traumatized victim becomes functional enough to hold down a simple job they can move into the homes provided by Faith Communities. This would save organizations like Covenant House a lot of money that they are now spending on transitional housing and that money could be used to take in more kids who need to be in a lock down facility. Teens and young adults are resilient. They often thrive once they get adult intervention, it just takes patience. While institutional models are necessary, everyone needs friends, family, community support. Only places of worship can provide that to these kids through a model similar to the Regenisis model. Compared to institutional models, it is far more cost effective for a faith community to take this on because faith communities have volunteers.

The Regenisis model or the "Children of the Night" model may be too big a "bite" for many churches to start with. The "Open Table" model may be more practical and could easily be used for a homeless kid in need. (www.theopentable.org) A group of around twelve volunteers come alongside an impoverished family or homeless kid for a year. They bring their vocational and life experiences along with their personal networks to mentor that family and help them develop a "life plan." In other words, they would use their personal networks to help the family or homeless kid find a job and their personal skills to mentor the family/kid on practical skills like budgeting. The people who serve are often the ones who get the most out of this program and their enthusiasm for the program is evoking a lot of interest in this model.

Religious organizations will feel the need to bring God into a kid's life, to share the comfort they know is available to a kid who is suffering. However you will find that many of these kids do not believe in God. They feel that if there is a God, how could He have allowed them to be raped, beaten, etc.?! For this reason, you will need to be patient. The motto of organizations that have been successful at bringing God into a kid's life is "Relationship before Religion," meaning you need to make it safe for the kids to process, at the rate at which they are able to process, all that has happened to them before many can even consider that there might be a God who loves them. By you acting as the representative of that love, by being there for them, it is most often that relationship that brings them to God. *(6.7)*

If you are an "advocate" type, you can go to the various websites that have campaigns like https://www.dosomething.org/facts/11-facts about-homeless-teens and use social networking to raise awareness. Teens are in high demand for sex trafficking. We need to get them off the street! Once these kids age and we see them on the street as adults, we lose sympathy for them. We need to remember that the homeless adults we see are often former "lost kids." The earlier we can intervene in someone's life, the better their chances at turning their life around.

References: (6.1) Conversation with an OC social worker.
(6.2) Conversation with CASA staff member
(6.3) Conversation with Olivecrest staff member
(6.4) Conversation with CASA staff member
(6.5) Conversation with Big Brothers and Sisters staff member
(6.6) Special agent for Homeland Security
(6.7) Staff member from www.BuildFutures.org

CHAPTER SEVEN

Reduce the Demand by Ending Pornography Addiction

While we have always had prostitution, many are of the opinion that the porn addiction pandemic is creating an increased demand for child prostitutes and victims of all ages. *(7.1)* Many of you will want to skip this chapter because the whole idea of pornography is so distasteful. This very avoidance is one of the reasons why pornography addiction is skyrocketing. Others of you truly hate pornography and have been unclear on how to fight it. For you, this chapter will be the most valuable in this book. The purpose of this chapter and Chapter Eight is to break down what needs to be done so anyone can fight the prevalence of pornography. By doing that, then millions can join the fight and it will take millions to stop porn from contributing to divorce, endangering our kids and creating a demand for sex trafficking victims.

Any General knows that you are more likely to win the war if you can take the fight to more than one "front." This chapter will address fighting porn on four fronts. First, we need to encourage our law enforcement entities to aggressively prosecute porn producers who are producing illegal porn. Second, we need to establish that porn is a drug so that we can bring to bear all the restrictions we have for drugs, such

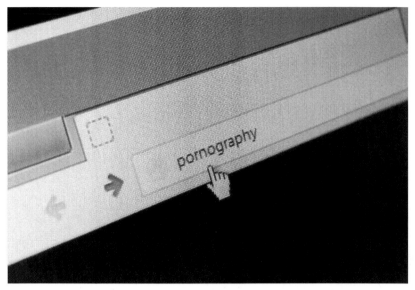

Viewing porn produces endorphins, making it very addicting.

as laws that prevent children from accessing it. *(7.2)* Third, we need to establish how linking sex and violence in the brain, is driving up the incidents of violence towards women. *(7.3)* Once we establish that violent porn is linked to many social problems, then actions will be taken to limit it. Fourth, we need to protect our children from accessing porn.

While studies show that unemployment, cultural values and drug addiction all contribute to domestic violence; violent porn may be another contributor. Domestic violence has become a pandemic in the U.S. The United States Office on Violence against Women (OVW) claims a woman is beaten every nine seconds with three women killed per day from having been assaulted. *(7.4)* We need definitive studies that establish a link between domestic violence, sexual assault, etc. and the prevalence of violent porn in order to encourage more of those fighting against violence toward women to join in the fight against violent porn. A great site for legislative actions to combat sexual violence is www.rainn.org.

Chapter Eight takes the fight to four additional "fronts." It includes resources to help rehabilitate porn addicts, advocacy/legislative action, the "opt in" campaign and the campaign to have every internet provider in the world block child porn at the provider's site before it can come into the country, like England has done. In order to win the battle against porn, we need to include as many people as possible in the fight. By taking on fighting porn on eight "fronts," we increase the number of people engaged in the fight as some people will be motivated by the idea of reducing the demand for Sex Trafficking, others by the "violence" aspect of porn, others will be motivated to protect their children, etc.

Before we go into the strategy we can take to reduce the demand for sex trafficking, let's look at why the demand for children is growing, despite the fact that child porn is illegal. Below are statistics that every-one should know which are posted at the "Enough is Enough" website (www.enough.org) regarding child pornography. You can go to the "Enough" site and in the left hand menu, select statistics to find the latest information on trends, etc.

•Child pornography is one of the fastest growing businesses online, and the content is becoming much worse. In 2008, Internet Watch Foundation found 1,536 individual child abuse domains. (Internet Watch Foundation. Annual Report, 2008).

•Of all known child abuse domains, 58 percent are housed in the United States (Internet Watch Foundation. Annual Report, 2008).

•The fastest growing demand in commercial websites for child abuse is for images depicting the worst type of abuse, including penetrative sexual activity involving children and adults and sadism or penetration by an animal (Internet Watch Foundation. Annual Report, 2008).

•In a study of arrested child pornography possessors, 40 percent had both sexually victimized children and were in possession of child por-nography. Of those arrested between 2000 and 2001, 83 percent had images involving children between ages 6 and 12; 39 percent had images of children between ages 3 and 5; and 19% had images of infants and toddlers under age 3 (National Center for Missing & Exploited Children, Child Pornography Possessors Arrested in Internet-Related Crimes: Findings from the National Juvenile Online Victimization Study. 2005.)

•Child pornography has become a $3 billion annual industry (Top

Ten Reviews, 2005) (End of stats from "Enough is Enough")

Since child and obscene porn is illegal, we can eliminate it through prosecution. However porn addiction most often starts with accessing legal porn. The problem is that legal porn is in the domain of "free speech," which restricts our ability to pass laws to limit it. Throughout history, all historic changes have been made by shifting the context/domain the issue is in. That is accomplished by changing public perception. *(7.5)* At one time in U.S. history, slavery was justified with the Bible and was acceptable. Over time that perception changed and slavery shifted from the context of a justifiable form of labor to the context of a great injustice and when the perception changed, people's actions changed. If we are successful at getting legal porn out of the context of "free speech" and into the context/domain of an addiction and/or a threat to persons, then we can strengthen our current laws regarding porn.

In this chapter we will review what it takes to change public perception in order to shift context, but first let's clear up the confusion regarding what is legal and what is not. Let's start by over simplifying it. There is clearly illegal pornography as in child porn or actually killing someone on film or stabbing them, acts involving torture and/or extreme degradation like sex with animals, etc. There is clearly legal pornography such as your standard x rated seduction and mating type porn. Then there is everything in between that may or may not be illegal.

The FCC makes the distinction between obscenity and indecent material. The FCC regulates TV in the U.S. and according to their rules, obscenity can never be shown. Indecent cannot be shown between the hours of 6 A.M. and 10 P. M. Indecent is that which does not rise to the level of obscenity and indecent is protected by "Free Speech." On the FCC website their standard for obscenity is posted which is: "According to the U.S. Supreme Court, to be obscene material must meet a three-prong test: (1) an average person, applying contemporary community standards, must find that the material, as a whole, appeals to the prurient interest (i.e., material having a tendency to excite lustful thoughts); (2) the material must depict or describe, in a patently offensive way, sexual conduct specifically defined by applicable law; and (3) the material, taken as a whole, must lack serious literary, artistic, political, or scientific value. The Supreme Court has indicated that this test is designed to cover hard-core pornography." (End post from FCC website) According to the law, if material is deemed obscene then it is illegal to distribute or sell and can carry fines and up to 5 years in prison.

In the U.S. we have been successful at convicting illegal porn producers; however in recent years we have become lax in our efforts to prosecute illegal porn. So the first action we need to take is to ask our law enforcement entities to "step up" the campaign to prosecute producers of illegal/obscene porn. The second action we could take is to establish porn as a drug so we can restrict legal porn as we do with all drugs, especially blocking a child's ability to access it. The fact is that watching videos of pornography produces endorphins, is addicting and leads to perversion. You can get a complete report on how porn affects the brain at www.fightthenewdrug.org and select "Get the Facts," and then select "The Brain."

In the U.S. we did try to prevent children from accessing porn by passing the "Child Online Protection Act" in 1998. COPA would have made it a crime to knowingly post material that is "harmful to minors" on the web for "commercial purposes" without having some method -- such as a credit card -- to verify a visitor's age. *(7.6)* However, the Act was overturned in 2008 in the name of "free speech." If we are successful at taking porn out of "free speech," and into the domain of an addiction, then we can get a law like this passed, as we do protect kids from addictive substances.

What many do not realize is that after a while the porn user becomes desensitized to the same content and no longer receives the stimulation the user is seeking, so without exception addicts will seek sites that are increasingly more violent, with younger and younger victims, which is why we have the statistics depicted from enough.org. Sex therapist Victor B Kline describes the process of porn addiction this way.... "In this phase, (3rd phase) material that was originally perceived as unthinkable, shocking, illegal, repulsive, or immoral is now viewed as acceptable and commonplace by the viewer of pornography. Regardless of the deviancy expressed, the viewer perceives the pornography and his or her use of it as legitimate. (4th phase) ……..Then the user moves to acting out what they see." (7.7) This scenario is literally creating legions of new pedophiles and violent rapists.

After watching hundreds, maybe thousands of hours of violent sex and sex with children/teens, it rewires the brain (7.8) and the individual can become impotent in healthy sexual situations. They then need the stimulus of violence or being with children and walk around with a compulsion that needs an outlet. In order not to get caught, they seek out pimps who will provide what they need. If they can't afford to use a pimp, they will find their victims in other ways.

The statistics from "Enough is Enough" tell us that pornography is becoming increasingly more violent. Linking the sex drive, which is one of the strongest drives we have, to violence is a volatile combination. Young women complain about how sexually aggressive men have become. One in four women will be sexually assaulted on a college campus. (7.9) Women are complaining about what their partners are expecting them to do while having sex. To the porn user, violent and depraved acts become "normalized" if they have spent hours viewing it. The report on how "Porn Affects Behavior" from the website www.fightthenewdrug.org goes into detail on this. Sex trafficking victims share that prostitutes are being beaten to death. Organizations that take care of street kids will tell you that street kids take speed and walk all night and sleep during the day because they don't dare sleep at night given how dangerous the streets are at night. (7.10) Those addicts for whom violence and/or murder is a sexual stimulus are looking for these kids.

Any speech act that encourages harm against another is considered "hate speech." You can Google "how hate crimes limit free speech" to understand how many speech acts that were once "free speech" and legal are now under "hate speech" and illegal. Many countries have similar legislation regarding hate speech that the U.S. has. A clever attorney could use the precedent we have established with hate speech legislation to create an argument for many acts of violent porn to come under "hate" speech. Many groups feel that violent porn is encouraging violence against women. So the third action we can take is to put legal violent porn under "hate speech" legislation in order to get rid of the violent porn that does not reach the level of illegal/obscene porn.

The argument over the question "Does watching violence encourage violence against another?" has been going on for years with regard to violent video games for kids. They found that some kids did become more violent after playing violent games, but not enough to justify eliminating violent video games. *(7.11)* However, games do not link the power of the sex drive, to violence in the brain. The harm that has been done to others, as a result of linking sex and violence together needs to be considered in any campaign to reduce porn. At a recent High School presentation, "Fight the New Drug" shared about teenage boys who were hitting their girlfriends during sex because in the porn they had viewed, the women liked it. The Witherspoon Institute reported that "23% of the 200 prostituted women that they interviewed had been assaulted by clients seeking porn sex who "insisted that the women enjoyed the assault. *(7.12)* From here, it is a short step to domestic violence.

Many are resigned and feel that with violent porn, porn producers can "spin" the case for producing violent porn by claiming the acts are part of the story and would be acceptable according to community standard because our society has become so sexualized and violent. The fact is that when put in front of a jury, cases are won against the majority of cases that have been prosecuted as most people do not feel that violent porn is acceptable according to "community standards." So even though "porn is everywhere," we need to snap out of our resignation and become more aggressive at fighting it.

What about all the porn that encourages adults having sex with teens? One of the reasons "Porn Harms Dirty Dozen" put Verizon on their list is because Verizon announced they were offering teen based porn as part of their "pay per view" with titles such as "I Banged My Stepdad," and "Pigtailed Teens Pounded." *(7.13)* Porn producers take short, thin 18 year olds and make them look like they are teens and have them act as the great seductress. Yes, this is legal if the actress is actually 18 because they are showing a "story" about a teen seducing an older man and they are not using a *real* teen. However, if put in front of a jury, the jury may feel that "teen" porn does violate community standards, so we need to take it to the people.

If these videos showed teens being victimized that would be one thing, but what they often show is the teens being the seductress. What idea is that putting into people's heads?! Shouldn't teen porn be considered "hate speech," if it is encouraging adults to have sex with teens, even if the actor/actress is 18 or older? The Los Angeles police will tell you that the average age a kid is being prostituted in Los Angeles is now 13 and they expect it to reach 12 by the end of 2014 and that is average!

In June of 2014, Porn Harms announced that their campaign against Verizon's FIOS TV offerings was successful and Verizon removed teen based porn from FIOS. Verizon is to be commended for their action to remove offensive porn as it costs them a lot of money to do that. Many companies make "Porn Harms Dirty Dozen" list and other internet/phone provider may also be profiting from porn. What we need to do is keep going to the "Porn Harms" site and whenever any company makes the list, bring that to the attention of our groups and invite them to use the Porn Harms site to sign their petitions or write to the companies on the "Dirty Dozen" list. If there is enough outrage brought against the worst offenders, hopefully they will rethink their actions like Verizon did. If they go off the list, we should also write them and commend them for their actions.

In order to take actions two and three, we need to understand the "free speech" aspect of porn. Just like all speech acts are not the same, all porn is not the same. We need to take violent and degrading porn that does not reach the level of illegal/obscene and porn that encourages sex with teens out of "free speech." Unless we take the most offensive legal porn out of "Free Speech," then we won't win the battle or the war as many attempts to limit legal porn have been overturned in the name of "free speech." COPA and porn in libraries are two examples of this. Many attempts to get porn out of libraries have been made by citizen groups, only to lose in court because legal porn is considered "Free Speech." (More on this Chapter Eight.)

There is another aspect in the campaign to limit porn that we need to consider, in taking on the worst that is out there. So far we have been referring to pictures and videos but human beings can use their imagination to create their own "pictures" simply by reading content. I inadvertently purchased a book at an airport that was about an uncle and his affair with his 10 year old niece. I got a few pages into the book because it took me awhile to understand that what I was reading was the story of a pedophile abusing a child. The reason why it took me awhile is because it was the child who came on to the uncle (not the other way around) and both were thoroughly enjoying the act. I thought there was a typo in the book regarding the child's age because I couldn't believe that I had bought a book like that at an airport!

Through further research, I learned three things from that experience. One is that stores may not know what they are selling and we should let them know if we find something that is inappropriate. The second thing I learned is that pedophiles feel totally justified in doing what they are doing. They have global networks where they share images, fantasies, techniques and sometimes real children. *(7.14)* They have been brainwashed into thinking that the children "want and enjoy" the sex. The reality is that for an adult to have sex with a child, it tears the vaginal/intestinal wall *(7.15)* and is a form of torture. Surgeons will tell you that it is often not possible to make whole again, a kid who has been repeatedly abused. The third thing I learned is that if seducing a child is part of your fictional or true story line for a movie or book, you can use it as long as you don't show pictures because the pictures are child porn and illegal, the story is not. This loophole only applies to books and movies when they are telling a story.

There was an arrest for a "How To" book which is in a different category than a fictional story. Philip R. Greaves II was arrested for selling his book "Pedophile's Guide to Love and Pleasure: A Child — Lover's Code of Conduct." However he was only sentenced to 2 years' probation! If you are confused by his sentence it is because he wasn't convicted for having sex with children which does carry prison sentences. He was convicted for writing a "How To" book. *(7.16)*

While there may be a legitimate reason as part of the story to include child seduction, we should still require that stories without pictures cannot graphically give tips on how to seduce children or suggest that the child enjoyed the sex. I can "hear" people screaming "Creative License." However, even with "Creative License," the current legislation on "Hate Speech," limits what one can write or say about a person's race, religion, ethnicity, nationality, gender, sexual orientation, gender identity and disability. In other words, if you want to establish your character as a racist, you can have them talk in a way so that people get the idea. However, you can't go on for pages as to what is wrong with the race your character is referring to in such a way that would encourage harm to them. That would be considered creating "bias" against a specific race and is illegal. So we need to include books with no pictures that encourage child seduction as part of a "hate speech" campaign against porn.

I have read the arguments from the media about violence being part of the story in the film, but they can still have their story and tone down the violence. The movie can show screaming behind closed doors with the actor talking later to a co-actor about how they beat their victim. For any porn producer who is reading this who isn't producing films with the scenes depicted on the preceding pages and doesn't want to be associated with producers who are encouraging the degradation of women and teen abuse, then you should form an association of porn producers who are not producing these types of films.

One of the concerns in fighting porn is the cost of prosecution. Through asset seizure and fines that are collected from convicted porn producers, an aggressive effort to fight porn could be profitable for the state. We could also consider establishing a system of fines for weak cases that prosecutors may be reluctant to prosecute and then move to prosecution for repeat offenders. Given that producing porn is about greed, it makes sense to establish stiff fines for porn that may not reach the level of illegal/obscene like teen based porn.

Part of the problem we have in getting people motivated to fight pornography is that we greatly underestimate how often someone is raped or how often a child is molested because of all the shame around molestation and rape. A rape victim does not want people to know they have been raped. If a child has been molested, that family is going to keep that a secret, as they know that once people know, they will treat that child differently. Also, the family also does not want grandpa or an uncle to go to prison. *(7.17)* All the secrecy is leading people to believe that rape and child molestation are rare. The National Center for Missing and Exploited Children tells us that 1 in 5 women and 1 in 10 boys will be sexually victimized.

In order to encourage our Attorney Generals to become more aggressive about prosecuting illegal porn producers, we need to speak up! For those of you who want all porn eliminated, that battle does not look like it can be won any time soon. However, we can succeed at mounting a campaign to aggressively prosecute illegal porn and limit the most objectionable material that is currently legal and we can do a better job of protecting our children. So how do we establish porn as a drug and limit violent porn? The answer is, we get the media to "talk it up" the consequences of porn addiction and how violent porn affects behavior.

Kids and Porn

What is really disturbing is the marketing that is being done to seduce teens into the world of pornography. It is rare to find a teen that has not had some exposure to pornography. We may have a lock on our own computers but kids can now use their cell phones, itouch, their tablets and pads, etc. unless we block them. The result is that we have teens and young children acting out what they see with their younger siblings and friends, as they are too immature to understand the consequences of their actions. We really need parents, teachers, Boy Scout leaders, our youth group leaders at our places of worship, our schools etc. to be talking about how destructive pornography is.

You can ask your school to invite www.fightthenewdrug.org to come do their presentation, "Porn Kills Love." They are awesome! On

The average age a child starts viewing porn is 8.

their "About" tab at their site, they assert that "We are the first generation in the history of the world to face the issue of pornography to this intensity and scale. We're also the first generation with a fact-based understanding of the harm that pornography can do and with that knowledge, we feel the responsibility to share it with others." One of the things we can do to protect our children is to support organizations like this that are successfully reaching out to the youth.

Teens are far more vulnerable to becoming addicted to porn, since a teen's brain reward pathway has a response two to four times more powerful than an adult brain, which means teen brains release even higher levels of dopamine. *(7.18)* Once the public accepts that porn addiction can do as much damage as any other drug addiction, we will have the power to limit a kid's access to porn. We don't let kids under the age of 21 drink, because an immature kid who is drunk can do a lot of damage. Well, an immature kid under 21 who has viewed any type of porn, especially violent porn can and has done a lot of damage.

LONDON, March 4, 2013 (LifeSiteNews.com) – "Pornography and depictions of sexuality have turned more than 4,500 British children –

some of them as young as five – into sexual offenders, according to a UK-based child welfare charity." This stat is over a 3 year period and most likely refers to kids who molested other people's kids because families will keep sibling sex abuse a secret, which means this statistic is probably low. The U.S. has six times the population of the U.K. and we have more and more children committing sex crimes as a result of being exposed to porn. If the media did enough programs on sex and violent crimes done by kids as a result of viewing porn, there would be an overwhelming demand to set up systems to keep kids away from porn so we need to ask them to do that.

An eye opening article written by John Woods, a psychotherapist at The Portman Clinic describes the process of how kids will go to one site and as a result of clicking on "pop ups" will wind up at extremely violent sites. "Pop ups" are compelling. It is difficult to refrain from "clicking" on them, especially with provocative titles that suggest that if one "clicks" on the "pop-up" they will be taken to an even more exciting site. Some "pop-ups" take users to child porn sites which the police monitor and these kids wind up being arrested as sex offenders and they are only 13! *(7.19)*

Luke Malone wrote an article entitled "You're 16. You're a Pedophile. You Don't Want to Hurt Anyone. What Do You Do Now?" The article tells the story of a 16 year old who became addicted to child porn and in order to protect kids from being hurt by him, he decided the only way out was to commit suicide. He couldn't' tell anyone his dark secret. *(7.20)* How many thousands of kids are living in anguish because of porn addiction that started with porn being sent to them on their phones?! We really need to push for the "Opt In" campaign in every country in the world which would block *all* porn unless one "opts in." Iceland's motivation for establishing this "business regulation" in their country is that they feel this is the most expedient way to protect children from porn.

There are news stories that address kids viewing porn where people are allowed to comment and many comments include statements to the effect… "parents need to do a better job of talking to and monitoring their kids." These people are clearly not parents. I know many parents who have talked to their kids, have kept the computer in the family room so they can monitor their child's online activity, have synced their child's cell phone to the "Cloud" so they can monitor what their children are viewing on their cell phone, etc. only to have the kid at the lunch table next to their child, hand their child a cell phone with the latest porn video. This is happening at grammar schools. One parent asked her 6th grader if the kids at school talked about porn. She expected him to respond with "What is porn?" Instead, he said "Oh yeah, mom. Every day at lunch, all the kids are talking about it!"

I have talked to weeping parents who did everything right, had their kids in bible study, attended their sports games, ate dinner together, etc. only to have their kids taken out of their home in handcuffs because at a young age someone handed their pre-teen porn and they acted out what they saw. So many lives destroyed including the victim, the perpetrator and the families of both as in this example: "11/98 - 11-year-old Josh had been looking at graphic violent porn on the Internet for 20 minutes immediately before stabbing 8-year-old Maddie Clifton to death." (Dangerous Access, 2000)

If you want a guide to help you talk to your kids about porn, then go to wwwpornharm.com/handouts and select "click here to access graphics, presentations," etc. and select the "Help for Addressing with Kids," icon and download "The Guideline." If you are looking for resources to familiarize yourself with the sexual culture our kids are a part of beginning at the middle school level, you can read Josh McDonnell's position paper at www.just1clickaway.org. According to his site, as many as 90% of kids 8 and older have accessed porn, often while doing homework. At a presentation at a local school that was done by the police, they demonstrated that looking up something as mundane as "milk" can lead one to porn sites. (If you look up "milk" in the "Urban Dictionary," it describes the sex act associated with the word "milk.")

Whenever I do a presentation, one of the questions I am often asked is "How do I block my kid's devices?" Simple, just Google, "How do I block porn from (name of device)" and you will get step by step instructions. You can ask your cell phone provider how to view your children's browsing history, texts, etc. However the police and Homeland Security will tell you that clever kids know how to get around blocks on their phone and other devices. You can find a video on how to do almost anything on You-Tube, including sites on how to unblock, blocked porn sites. These videos are hosted by hackers who boast about their abilities. You should still block your children's devices and check them from time to time to make sure they are still blocked.

Vanguard University's "Ending Human Trafficking" podcast #67, offers suggestions for protecting your kids like using www.opendns.com. If you click on Home Parental Controls at their site, you can set up your home network so that no device in your home can access porn, gambling or whatever you may object to. This includes your children's cell phones when they use your wireless router. What many people don't realize is that the program on their computer to block porn only blocks that computer. Their kids could be in the other room accessing porn on their cell phones, etc. The most likely time a kid will watch porn is late at night when their parents are asleep, so take away their cell, ipad, power cord to their gaming system and computer, etc. before you go to sleep. Don't forget their gaming systems as those systems have internet access. Even if they are not watching porn, they could be texting their friends at three in the morning which you don't want either.

Keeping kids away from porn and doing a better job of toning down the violent content is a battle that can be won, because the majority of the public want that. We just haven't organized ourselves sufficiently to take action. So let's get to work!

References: (7.1) www.stoptraffickingdemand.com. "Johns Acting Out" under the "Facts" tab and Porn Harms research section.
(7.2)(7.3) www.fightthenewdrug.org. Under "Get the Facts, (7.2) Article entitled "Porn is Like a Drug. (7.3) Article entitled "Porn Effects Your Behavior."
(7.4) The Washington Times Communities. "Domestic Violence is not Only on the Rise, It is a Pandemic." Paul Mountjoy 5.21.13
(7.5) Book "Three Laws of Performance," by Steve Zafron and David Logan. "Rewriting a Chapter That's Already Written

(7.6) abcnews.go.com/Technology/AheadoftheCurve/Child Online Protection Act Overturned." July 23rd, 2008

(7.7) Victor B. Cline, "Pornography and Sexual Addictions," Christian Counseling Today 4, no.4 (1996)

(7.8) Research section of <u>www.pornharms.com</u>, "Porn and Sexual Violence." Article posted from Business Standard. "Porn Addiction Triggering Rise in Sex Crimes" Ians. 5.22.14

(7.9) Christian Science Monitor, "At Colleges Plagued by Date Rape, Why "no," Still Means "yes." 6.28.2011

(7.10) Conversation with Covenant House staff member.

(7.11) Psych Central. "In New Study, Video Games not Tied to Violence in Youth" Rick Nauert, 8.27.13

(7.12) www.stoptraffickingdemand.com. "Johns Acting Out"

(7.13) Fox News, "Verizon Defends Decision to offer Incest and Child Themed Porn on Video on Demand. 3.20.14

(7.14) Ernie Allen, co-founder of Missing and Exploited Children, speaker for Vanguard's 2012 Human Trafficking Conference.

(7.15) Ashley Judd, from the conversations she had with Aid's workers in her book "All That Is Bitter & Sweet: A Memoir."

(7.16) Orlando Sentinel Oct 13, 2013. " Phillip R. Greaves II: Author of pedophile guide sentenced to probation."

(7.17) Conversation with an L.A Police Officer

(7.18) Article entitled "Porn is Addictive." At www.fightheillegaldrug.org.

(7.19) Mail Online News, April 29, 2012 "Jamie is 13 and hasn't even kissed a girl. But he's now on the Sex Offender Registry after online porn warped his mind..."

(7.20) Link for the article https://medium.com/matter/youre-16-youre-a-pedophile-you-dont-want-to-hurt-anyone-what-do-you-do-now-e11ce4b88bdb

CHAPTER EIGHT

Resources for Porn Addicts and Legislative Action

According to the Christian Broadcasting Network, (www.cbn.com) this addiction poses the greatest threat to the American Family today. Where we are at with pornography addiction is similar to where we were at with alcoholism before AA started in 1934. Like alcoholics in the 1930's, porn addicts keep their addiction a secret. We need to break through the denial that is keeping people trapped. The shame associated with porn addiction and the reluctance to speak up has created a public perception that seriously underestimates how widespread this addiction is and is keeping addicts from seeking help.

Many are under the misconception that watching videos is similar to having a Playboy magazine and "boys will be boys." Many completely underestimate the effects on behavior that watching hundreds of hours of videos produces. How do you know if you are addicted? Simple, you view pornography almost every day and it has become a regular part of your life. *(8.1)* This addiction is harder to overcome than drug addiction, because with drugs you can remove the drug. With pornography addiction you can remove one's computer, but people can continue to run the videos in their head and never really be free. *(8.2)*

Resources for Porn Addicts

You can use the search engine at the Christian Broadcasting Network site to find Christian resources for help. This site also has several shows that one can watch. What is powerful about their resources is one can listen to the testimony of decent guys sharing how pornography has ruined their marriages and negatively affected their lives. Listening to testimonies is a far more powerful motivator for porn addicts to get help than quoting statistics. You can show clips from one of these shows at a speaking engagement that you set up. Another great resource is www.unearthedpictures.org, which has some awesome films by men for men that speak to the whole dynamic of porn, its attraction, underlying causes of why men seek prostitutes, etc. What is great about "Unearthed" and "Fight The New Drug" is these sites are hosted by young people whose generation has been the most impacted by porn.

Another great resource for families is www.safefamilies.org. (The site for keeping children out of the foster care system has a dash (-) between safe and families like this, www.safe-families.org so you don't get confused.) Safe Families offers free software tools for parents, a Q & A to find out if you are addicted, guidelines for parents on social networking, media savvy advice and a special section for pastors if they have been tempted. This site makes the point that for Pastors who have viewed pornography, they may feel especially trapped. They fear that if they admit it, it will undermine the faith of the people around them. The amount of detail and resources at this site for church leaders to help themselves and/or help the members of their church is very, very well thought out.

Given the shame associated with porn addiction, it is not something addicts feel comfortable talking about but they will bring it up in the confessional. For that reason, Father Stephen Joseph Rosetti has written books for priests on how to counsel individuals who confess this sin. It is a great resource for any faith leader who encounters this issue.

www.purerestoration.com offers workshops entitled "Every Man's Battle," a 3 day intensive program offered all over the country to explore the area of Sexual Integrity. In addition to offering this workshop, New

Life Ministries assists over 10,000 callers each month in finding workshops, outpatient counselors, books, and other resources to meet their needs. (800-639-5433) They are the nation's largest provider of Christian counseling services with nearly 1000 licensed counselors in more than forty states, offering individual and family counseling for every need.

Many faith communities are doing a "White Ribbon" campaign to raise awareness. Canada has a "White Ribbon" campaign as a protest against violence to women.   That campaign could easily be combined with the one that you can find at a "WRAP" site which stands for "White Ribbon Against Pornography."   All you have to do for the "White Ribbon" event is set up a table, have the person leading the service do a short announcement letting people know your table is out there and pass out white ribbons and information that you can find at a "WRAP" site.

If you go to www.pornharms.com and scroll to the bottom, you will find many categories of resources that you could use for your event.   If you are looking for handouts, graphics, etc. for a WRAP campaign, then go to http://pornharms.com/handouts.   The announcement and table need to be promoted in such a way that a porn user could come up and get information anonymously. In other words, you could promote that you have information on how to protect kids, resources for porn addicts and their partners, flyers with information on how porn changes the brain, etc. Then an individual can come up to the table and take "one of each," so it just looks like they are interested without revealing themselves as an addict.

In addition to the addict themselves, we need to consider the many, many women who are married to or are girlfriends of men who are porn addicts.   Sometimes these women have to deal with their partner molesting their own children. We need groups for these women so they can help themselves and their spouse or boyfriend.   In response to this need, churches have set up "COSA" groups. "COSA" stands for "Codependent Women in Relationship with Sexually Addicted Men."   These groups are often an extension of the "Celebrate Recovery" program offered at many churches that is making such a huge difference in the healing of so many lives, so many marriages. "Celebrate Recovery" is in 20,000 churches (www.celebraterecovery.com) and the leaders will come to your faith community to train your volunteers on how to set it up. *(8.3)*

Often people who have been victims of domestic violence, child abuse, etc. are drawn to work on trafficking issues as they feel empathy for the victims because of what they went through. It is always a good idea to heal oneself first before you attempt to heal others. Otherwise, the association with trafficking victims may open old wounds. Another program to consider is the Landmark Forum. While not a faith based program, in 3 days the Landmark Forum provides the opportunity to be free of the suffering that one is carrying from past abuse. (www.landmarkworldwide.com)

Advocacy and Legislative Action

We need both a "top down" and "bottom up" approach that engages both government and the average individual to fight porn. There are some great sites that have made it easy for individuals to engage in the fight. Everyone can go to www.fightthenewdrug.org and take the pledge and join the "Street Team." At www.pornharms.com, you can select the "Projects" tab and find a project to get involved in. If you are interested in doing a conference to educate your community, then at this same site, scroll down under "Projects" and select "Ignite the Light" for information on local conferences and how to organize an interfaith conference in your area. In addition to these public conferences, Morality in Media will help ensure that church leadership is also trained on the subject. MIM has been fighting this issue since 1962 and is considered the leading organization opposing porn through education and application of the law. In addition to "Porn Harms," Morality in Media has another great site with lots of resources, entitled "War on Illegal Porn." (http://waronillegalpornography.com)

We can all write to the media and ask for their help to raise awareness regarding the effects of violent porn on our society and establish that porn is a drug. The media can host experts on their shows and quote studies. "Fight the New Drug" has many resources the media can use under "Get the Facts." We need the media to shift the way people think about porn if we are going to be successful at making changes.

What about kids being sold through online ads? The Attorney Generals from all of the states in the U.S. contacted many different publications where kids were being sold online through escort service type ads and asked those publications to stop running those types of ads. To their credit, Craig's list cooperated and eliminated their "adult" section. However many publications did not cooperate because they don't want to give up the revenues. If you want to find out more about this campaign, then go the site for the "Attorney General for California" and search for the "State of Human Trafficking in California, 2012 Report" and go to page 105 to review the letter sent to "BackPage.com." While it is illegal for the Traffickers to post ads that sell kids, publications are not responsible for monitoring what goes into the ads for their newspapers or websites. We need to craft laws that make publications socially responsible for posting ads that sell kids so they can't use the "free speech" defense.

The state of Washington did try to pass such a law with SB 6251 which would require publications to verify the age of the kids in their ads. This law was in response to the rescue of kids as young as 14 who had been "sold" through online ads with their picture! The law was drafted in January of 2012 and by December it was dropped by the state after the judge expressed this opinion.... "Whether or not Facebook (and other publications) already 'knows' that it is publishing such ads, if SB 6251 is enforced, Facebook will have a strong incentive to either ex-ante monitor content that is posted to its website or require blanket age verification before photos are uploaded to its site," Martinez wrote. "This kind of restriction could cause dangerous chilling effects across the Internet." *(8.4)*

I don't know about you but I would love to have those "dangerous chilling effects across the internet" so that we can protect kids! We don't need our publications to require blanket verification of age for all ads, but if the ads are for "Escort or Massage" then the ages should have to be verified. With regard to the "free speech" and the "first amendment" defense, let's keep in mind that if there is enough public outrage like there has been for "hate speech/crimes" we can take ads like this out of the domain of "free speech" and into the domain of "hate crimes" and get laws passed. The state of Washington is trying again to prevent minors from being sold through ads with the "SAVE" act. "The Stop Advertising Victims of Exploitation" act passed the House in May 2014 and is waiting for the Senate vote. Let's see if it gets challenged again in the courts. You can Google this act for updates.

What about libraries? Parents are stressed over the fact that viewers are watching porn in view of their children at our public libraries. Do we really want individuals watching porn and becoming sexually stimulated while being around our kids? Parents who can't afford after school care send their kids to libraries where they pick them up after work, thinking they are safe there.

Libraries have been sued for blocking access to porn in the name of "free speech" and libraries have backed down and allowed porn. However, the tide is starting to turn. The North Central Regional Library took the case to court and won. Judge Edward F. Shea in Spokane said "the North Central Regional Library district's policy on computer use does not violate patrons' First Amendment right to information." His summary stated that the library has the right to restrict what goes on its shelves and what can be accessed online. (8.5)

We need more judges like this who won't be intimidated by the "free speech" defense and make common sense decisions about protecting kids from porn. Everyone should ask their library if they are blocking porn sites and if not, get a group together and go to the county and insist that they do that. They can use the North Central Regional Library case as a precedent. At www.pornharms.com, select "Projects" at the top and then "Safe Schools, Safe Libraries" from the drop down menu. In the middle of the page you can find a "Getting Started" packet with the information you need to take action. On the same page, if you select "What are the Laws," you will find the current laws for libraries for your state.

We need to go to our cities and ask them to block porn at libraries.

Congress did pass the "Children's Internet Protection Act" in 2000 to encourage libraries to block porn, but it only "encourages" them to do that. We need to *insist* that our cities block porn at our libraries.

The porn producers have the money, but we have the power because there are more of us who do not want children exposed to porn, than there are people who will fight to make porn available to kids. The problem is that the current effort to protect kids from all porn is insufficient to get it done. Not enough people are "speaking up." We all need to get "in the ring" and take action.

We need our representatives to provide the kind of leadership that Prime Minister Cameron is providing. Prime Minister David Cameron made a move in July of 2013 to require that all internet providers block child porn so that no one in England can access it. He also added two other provisions in his personal campaign to fight porn. What his first provision means is that no one in England can access child porn through the internet, unless they are going into the "dark" web. However, I don't see too many teens and new porn addicts going into pedophile chat rooms to purchase the software to get into the "dark" web to purchase child porn when they never had access to child porn, to begin with. Cameron's second provision requires that all new computers block porn. What that means is that when one purchases a new computer, they won't be able to access porn on it, unless they go in and disable the filters. *(8.6)*

His third provision required that at the beginning of 2014, families had to let their internet provider know if they wanted to "opt in" to have access to porn. *(8.6)* Prime Minister Cameron jokes about wives finding porn on their computer and confronting their husbands about having "opted in." Cameron said "that conversation should be interesting." We should have "opt in" in every country in the world as that would make it possible for parents to check if other families have "opted in" before their children go over to their house to play. That would also be an interesting conversation!

What is brilliant about "opt in" is that it can't be overturned in the name of "free speech" because the request will be voluntary and it will bring people's porn usage into "the light." People will ask each other if they "opted in." People in the same household will know that if porn can be accessed on their computer, someone "opted in" and they can deal with that person. Faith Communities, parent groups, etc. will have the power to restrict porn by discouraging "opting in." It is too tempting to know one can access porn on one's computer. It is like having heroin in your house on a shelf where everyone, including your kids can access it. Removing the temptation will go a long way to reduce porn use.

If you read the various articles regarding Prime Minister Cameron's stand to block child porn you will find that in the beginning, he got push back from various groups. However, Prime Minister Cameron was unwilling to give up any ground on this, and to their credit Google and Microsoft went to work. In November of 2013 they agreed to block child porn worldwide. Using Microsoft (MSFT, Fortune 500) picture detection technology, a unique identification mark is applied to such content, and then all copies are immediately removed from the web. They cleaned up search results for over 100,000 web queries in over 150 languages and in many cases the user will get an online warning that child porn is illegal and offers advice on where to get help. *(8.7)* Now they are going one step further. In December of 2014 Google, Microsoft and Mozilla announced at the "We Protect Children Online" global summit that they would explore blocking child porn at the browser level meaning Explorer, Chrome and Firefox. *(8.8)* However, these three are not the only online browsers.

Now that we have the technology, all Internet search engines could be blocking child porn from coming into any country and given that child porn is illegal it begs the question, "why aren't they already doing that?!" The answer to that question is because we haven't demanded that they do so!! We need a march in every capitol in the world, where the press is invited, so we can draw more attention to the possibility that all search engines can block child porn at the provider's site and the power of the "opt in" campaign to protect our children from accessing porn. Most people do not know that these two options exist. If they did, there would be a public uproar demanding that the government institute these two regulations like Prime Minister Cameron did.

Morality in Media has a campaign (December 2013) to make "opt in" mandatory in the U.S. You will need to "click" on "View Latest Action Alerts" to the right, and enter "opt in" in the search bar to find the petition. (www.pornharms.com/petition-make-porn-opt-in-only/) The petition would require that all internet search engines block porn unless one calls their internet provider to "opt in." If restricting porn is an issue you are passionate about, then go to the "porn harms" site on a regular basis to support the many campaigns this group advocates for. Canada is advocating for "opt in" and Iceland is discussing blocking all porn access in their country. *(8.9)* Near the end of the book, in the section entitled "Supplement One" is a letter to the president that you can ask the media to use to raise awareness.

The way Prime Minister Cameron got around the "free speech" problem with his campaign to limit porn is that he made it a "business regulation" for his country. Governments can regulate businesses. The businesses themselves make policies as part of doing business. For instance, most companies don't allow employees to look at porn on company computers. In the United Kingdom, both McDonalds and Starbucks block porn through their Wi-Fi. *(8.10)* "Enough Is Enough" has several campaigns that they do, some of which are directed at businesses. Currently they are asking people to sign their petition to ask McDonalds and Starbucks to block their wifi porn in the U.S. Hopefully we can get that done before the end of 2014. "Enough" has several campaigns like this, so it is worthwhile to subscribe to their newsletter.

Prime Minister Cameron is to be commended for taking a stand against child porn. You will find in every story that relates to the kidnapping, rape and murder of a child, the perpetrator almost always was found with child porn. Child porn is the fastest growing aspect of the porn industry and the consequences are horrific. In small towns in Mexico, the gangs come to the houses of families and drag out their screaming 7 year old, leaving behind the weeping family and that child is never seen again. *(8.11)* This scenario is happening all over the world with the increased demand for child sex slaves. Let's join together in getting those pictures out of people's heads! The efforts of Google and Microsoft may or may not be sufficient, so we need to stay on top of this and keep speaking up until child porn is eliminated from the planet! We need to ask our faith leaders to raise awareness and use our social networks to ask people to petition all internet providers to block child porn in every country in the world.

The cost savings would be significant if we were successful in this effort to block child porn worldwide. We would save the cost of prosecuting offenders who go on child porn sites and the cost of having the police monitor child porn sites to catch them. More importantly, we would save children from horrific abuse and all the teens and men who started out as decent people who became addicts, who now live in a hell of their own making. There will still be offenders who will go into chat rooms and exchange child porn, but most pedophiles got started by going to sites that sent them to child porn sites, so any attempt to reduce child porn would significantly reduce the number of child predators.

In addition to eliminating child porn and limiting all other porn in the United Kingdom, in November of 2013 Prime Minister Cameron announced the partnership of the UK and the U.S. to enlist spy agencies to track down pedophiles who share images online. Cameron announced that the "...joint taskforce will work with encryption experts at Britain's GCHQ communications monitoring agency and the US National Security Agency (NSA) to find offenders who operate in the darkest corners of the Internet." *(8.12)* The majority of the internet is referred to as the "deep web" meaning you need special software to access it. In the "deep" web is the "dark" web where pedophiles and child porn addicts have their worldwide networks and buy and sell child pornography and children. Child porn addicts meet other addicts in chat rooms where they can get the software from each other. The "dark" web is also where the trafficking of illegal body parts happens. *(8.13)* This is why, in addition to taking on Google, Microsoft and the other internet search engines in the United Kingdom, Prime Minister Cameron took on the partnership with U.S. spy agencies, because these agencies have the ability to track down abusers in the "dark" web.

At the "We Protect Children Online" global summit that was attended by Internet firms and Social Networking sites like Facebook, Cameron announced new legislation that would close a loophole in the law. He introduced a bill to Parliament that would make it a crime to sexually solicit a child online. *(8.8)* Prime Minister Cameron's stand against porn has created an environment where limiting porn has become an "idea whose time has come." As a result, every month there are internet articles with the latest action a country or group has enacted or proposed to get done. If this is a subject you want to follow as well as find out the status of current laws in the U.S. regarding porn, then go to www.pornharms.com on a regular basis to get the latest updates. Better yet, create stories! At the Facebook pages of your favorite news host or talk show host, find a story that references porn in some way. Then have all your friends comment that we need "opt in" in the U.S. or your country. Show producers pay attention to what people seem to be interested in and if there are enough comments, they will consider doing a story. You can also often email reporters and suggest a story.

Our Attorney Generals and Government leaders like Prime Minister

Cameron are providing a "top down" approach to fighting porn. An example of a "bottom up" approach is the campaign by the "Family Research Council," to get porn off of college campuses. They are advocating for porn to be blocked from the dorms. They feel that since they are paying for their children's college education, they should have a vote on the type of environment their children are part of. *(8.14)* Another action to consider is to go directly to businesses that offer wi-fi and tell them to block porn and recommend that they promote the fact that they are doing that to enhance their brand. Once one company makes a change and the change becomes public and is well received, it starts a movement on the part of all companies to make the same change. Once people get it in their head that there are companies that are taking action to block porn, they will start asking all companies they do business with to do the same.

There are many efforts that different groups are taking on. One just needs to Google "who is fighting pornography?" We can ask the media to promote the efforts of groups who are fighting porn more "front and center." Hopefully this will encourage others to join the campaigns that many groups are taking on.

As individuals we can "vote with our money" by making sure we are not purchasing stocks that support a company that produces porn. You need to do research on any company whose product you purchase, to make sure they don't have a vested interest in the porn industry. If you want to get the attention of the publications that are advertising kids for sale through escort and massage ads, then Google "who owns (name of publication)." Write to them and let them know that your group, (call it the "Human Trafficking group of (name of faith community or organization)", is boycotting every product and service that company owns because of their ads advertising kids for sale in (name of) publication, unless they stop.

You always want to write to the publication first and give them an opportunity to respond to your letter before you recommend a boycott, because if you got the name of the corporation wrong and encourage people to boycott a company that is not doing what you claim they are doing, you can get sued so be careful with boycotting campaigns. You need to make sure you have your facts straight and only state what you can prove, like the publication advertises for escorts and you object to that. You can't claim that they are supporting Human Trafficking unless you know that for sure. Get several people to write. We can ask our Attorney Generals to do their "top down" part and we can do our "bottom up" part by putting enough pressure on publications so they voluntarily stop running those ads that sell people for sex.

We can ask our cities to go after those businesses that are involved in the commercial sex trade. If a "strip club" knows that if they set up shop in a particular city, that city is going to be aggressive about monitoring them for violations of the law, they will go someplace else. Cities can get a complete report of how to regulate businesses involved in the commercial sex trade by going to www.waronillegalpornography.com, select the "Laws" tab and then select "Opposing Local Sexually Oriented Businesses." Once you "click" on that link, if you scroll down to the bottom there are manuals for how to regulate several types of businesses.

If you feel motivated to write, then in addition to Porn Harms, "Dirty Dozen List of 12 Top Facilitators of Pornography Announced," you can also write to your representatives. Following are some suggestions that have been recommended by several groups, that need to be implemented. While it is illegal to be a prostitute, it is only a misdemeanor in the U.S. to have sex with a prostitute over the age of 18. We need to raise the age limit, so it is a felony to pay for sex with anyone under 21. We need to raise the legal age of a porn star to be 21. This would make it more difficult for a "client" to claim that they didn't know the girl/boy was a minor and harder to create "teen" type porn. We need laws in every state that prohibit businesses from putting together "Sex Tours."

We need to require that social media sites step up their efforts to monitor their sites for the solicitation and sale of kids and aggressively work with law enforcement to prosecute offenders. While we are at it, let's pass laws that get rid of all the chat rooms where pedophiles and Traffickers are exchanging and selling kids and giving each other "hot" tips on how to seduce children and how to avoid being caught. Somehow, we need to block the Traffickers ability to use the internet to sell kids. We need laws that prohibit publications from advertising on behalf of the Traffickers. Our representatives will respond if enough people get involved.

Under "Get Involved" at this site www.stoptraffickingdemand.com, you can select "Call Your Reps" or "Contact your Elected Representatives." There is list of suggestions of what you can talk to them about. You can meet with your local state assembly person or congressperson on any issue. You just need to get a group together and convince your representative that your group has influence and you will get a meeting. I am not suggesting that you make up how much influence you have, it needs to be true. I got a meeting by including in my group a representative from a local organization that had just had a meeting at a church where 1,000 people came and the event was in the newspaper. If you have a mega church in your area, you can ask the social outreach staff person to come and let your representative know that person will be one of the people in your group who will be at the meeting. If they think your group has influence, they will meet with you. However our representatives don't want to meet with some angry group who just wants to vent or treats them like the enemy and can only speak about how terrble the problem is.

Our representatives need solutions. So do your research, get your facts straight and make suggestions and talk to them like they are on your side, that they want what you want because they do. You can use what is in this book, but laws change all the time so make sure you have up to date information so you are credible. www.pornharms.com has an entire research section. Our representatives are looking for people to be resources for them so if you represent an organization and can give them "real life" examples of how this crime is being expressed in the community that they represent, they are very interested.

The campaign against porn will take persistence. There wasn't much "push back" for most of our 'hate crime" legislation because no one lost any money and there was no organized group who wanted to fight for the right to slander a particular race. The reason why it took a war to make slavery illegal was because of how much money slave owners were making. It will take a war of sorts to limit pornography because porn producers are making millions. They are organized and they will fight any attempt to limit them. Are you ready to get in there and fight?!

References:

(8.1) Dare to Dig Deeper booklet "Toxic Porn", by Gene McConnell and Keith Campbell. Focus on the Family.

(8.2) Conversation with counselor at Celebrate Recovery for sex addicts.

(8.3) From the "Celebrate Recovery" website. www.celebraterecovery.com

(8.4) Courthouse News Service, December 12, 2012. Washington Drops Online Sex Traffic Law. Nick McCann

(8.5) KING 5 News, Posted on April 10, 2012 at 4:56 PM. Eastern Wash. library district wins Internet filtering case against ACLU.

(8.6) Daily Mail. Blocks on internet porn to begin in new year: 20 million families will have to make a Yes or No choice on access to filth. By James Chapman. 11.15.13

(8.7) The Telegraph, 11.18.2013 "Google Vows to Block Child Pornography" by Haley Dixon. Also: The Washington Post "Google, Microsoft modify Internet searches to exclude more child pornography results." 11.18.2013 Hayley Tsukayama

(8.8) "I worry about my children online, says Cameron in call to web firms to do more to help spy agencies to catch pedophiles." Daily Mail.com, 12/11/14 Matt Chorley and David Chapman

(8.9) Huffington Post Oct 12, 2013. "Canadian Anti-Pornography Petition' Urges Opt-In Filter

(8.10) Post at www.enough.com

(8.11) Conversation with a friend who knows people who live in the towns in Mexico where this is happening.

(8.12) Bangkok Post, November 18, 2013 "US, UK enlist spy agencies to fight online child porn: PM" Online News World.

(8.13) CNN Money, "The Deep Web You Don't Know About. "3.10.14

(8.4) Interpacket News. Christian Lobbyists Fight To Eliminate Porn In College Dorms. July19, 2013.

CHAPTER NINE

Health Professionals, Teachers and Youth Pastors

f there was one thing I got really excited about when I did the research for this book was how many resources are available for teachers, youth pastors and health professionals. Human Traffickers are actively targeting teens. We need to counter that through the education of our youth. Health Professionals may be coming across victims of Human Trafficking and not even know it. Studies have shown that between 50 to 100 percent of surveyed trafficking survivors reported having received medical care when they were enslaved *(9.1)* It is important that health professionals, teachers and youth pastors educate themselves as to what to look for and what actions to take and to have the 888-3737-888 number programmed in their phones.

Nurses, Doctors, First Responders

Doctors and nurses are the most likely people to come across Trafficking victims because the Traffickers need their victims to be working and they can't work if they are sick or have been battered. If a victim of sex trafficking has an STD, it keeps her/him from working so sex trafficking victims could be coming in often. Labor victims may come in with back problems or other problems showing they are overworked.

At the Rescue and Restore website, the U.S. Department of Health and Human Resources offers great resources. The Rescue and Restore site (http://www.acf.hhs.gov) primarily focuses on outreach to those individuals who will most likely encounter victims on a daily basis, such as health care providers, social workers and law enforcement. On the tabs at the top, select "Programs," then "Human Trafficking," then "Tool Kits" to access the information for health professionals that is in both English and Spanish and includes information on how to understand the mindset of a trafficking victim, how to communicate with them and specific posters and brochures for Health Care Providers. The section of the program that outlines how to recognize a Trafficking victim would be useful for anyone to read. For example, it directs health care providers to look for individuals who appear to be controlled by another or when the patient is with a man or woman who does all the talking for them. This site has a list of questions that health professionals can ask their patients. Mainly they need to determine if the patient can leave their job and/or if they have been threatened or harmed in any way.

Vanguard University's "Ending Human Trafficking" podcasts #36 and #59 (available at iTunes) offer insight into the mindset of the victim. One of the presenters is Sandra Morgan, who is a former nurse. She does trainings for Health Care Providers and lets them know that Trafficking victims are brainwashed to be afraid of law enforcement, especially if they are here illegally. However they are more likely to open up to a caring health care provider, especially if that nurse or doctor knows the questions to ask and what actions to take.

It is important to keep in mind that victims have been brainwashed into thinking that their perpetrators have done nothing wrong. The pimp will often refer to his victim as his "girlfriend" and refer to his/her group of victims as the "family." Labor victims have been told that they are working off a debt so they may feel that there is some legitimacy to the way they are being treated. *(9.2)* It really takes skill to deal with this mindset to succeed in getting the victim to cooperate with you.

Sandra has suggestions regarding what types of education a health clinic, emergency rooms, etc. needs to provide. She recommends training the receptionist to look for women who come in often with a different group of men or women. If the patient does not seem to know the names of the group she came in with, that should make the receptionist suspicious. The receptionist needs training on how to skillfully separate the patient from his/her group as one would not want to do anything that makes the pimp (who could be a woman) suspicious. The receptionist can just tell the "handler" that no one can go in with the patient and then alert the nurse and/or doctor to their suspicions. However, the "handler" will insist on coming in with the patient. Victims are often forced to act like he/she cannot speak English or Spanish which becomes an excuse for a member of the group to be with the victim at all times to translate. Polaris tells us that if someone is looking to their translator for approval or seems afraid of the translator, you should be suspicious.

Health care professionals will have to come up with ways to get the patient alone, like telling the pimp/group that the patient needs an x-ray and the group will have to wait in the exam room and it will only take a minute. The Polaris Project has a fabulous "Comprehensive Trafficking

Alert Health Professionals have rescued many victims of Trafficking.

Assessment" tool that anyone on the front lines can use. It lets you know what to do in each situation. You can find it under "Resources" at their site. They also have materials in many different languages for use with someone you suspect might be a victim.

All of the resources mentioned so far are directed to health professionals at clinics or emergency rooms. Sandra Morgan reminds us to not forget school nurses who may be the first person a kid who has been solicited may see if they get an STD. Finding out how many partners a kid may have had, could be a red flag to ask more questions. The same holds true for pregnancy clinics. Some women who go to these clinics may be Trafficking victims and some may be young girls who are being "pimped out" by their boyfriend, including girls from "good" families who think they are in love. Health Professionals have always been good listeners, but we have been taught by society that asking a lot of personal questions is rude or inappropriate. Being assertive in asking the right questions may save someone from a life of degradation and servitude.

Teachers and Youth Pastors

Teachers, Youth Pastors and all those who work with teens are on the front lines to protect kids from all those who would exploit them. They would do well to review the list of questions that are recommended for health professionals. However, those questions are for kids who are already victims. Teachers and Youth Pastors are in a position to prevent victimization and need to be talking this up, so if a teen is being threatened or seduced, they will feel safe enough to approach that youth pastor or teacher to help them sort out if they are being exploited.

If a teacher or youth pastor is suspicious they can call either 911 or the Human Trafficking hotline. The Polaris Project will make suggestions and help them discern if there really is a problem. (1-888-3737-888) In the "Ending Human Trafficking" podcast #63, Sandra shares how one perceptive teacher noticed that the same student would leave early on Fridays and come in exhausted on Mondays so he asked her what she did on the weekends. Her answer was that she went to Las Vegas to "party" with friends. Upon further questioning, it was discovered that she was being used in the sex trade. One of the points the OC Human Trafficking Victims report made is that 70% of kids are recruited by someone they know. It could be a teen friend who tells them they know of a job where they can make great money.

If a teen is being "groomed" by a Trafficker, that teen is being exploited by a pro. They may be confused because they are in love but something does not quite feel right. They need help trying to discern what is going on and will most likely defend the "boyfriend" because they are viewing him with rose colored glasses. They want to believe that he thinks they are beautiful and that he is madly in love with them. Following is an example of a standard line that the Trafficker/boyfriend may use, that the lovesick teen believes..."Babe, you know I am trying to get a job but I just can't find one. You need to do this, because we need to eat (or something else they need). You know I love you baby. If it was the other way around, I would do it for you." *(9.3)*

To get started on any campaign to raise awareness regarding Human Trafficking, we need to start with education and given that everyone knows that educators are on the front line there are many programs for them. UNICEF has a complete lesson plan, one for grades 6-8 and another for grades 9-12 with over 40 pages. The lesson plan is complete with age appropriate stories of victims of Human Trafficking and age appropriate material explaining Human Trafficking. The UNICEF program addresses Trafficking all over the world. The A21 Campaign has a curriculum designed for High School educators to teach kids how to protect themselves entitled "Bodies are not Commodities." The curriculum is aligned to the Common Core State Standards and includes a supplementary curriculum for Social Studies and youth pastors. Under the "Get Involved" tab, (www.thea21campaign.org) just scroll down to "Education" to access it.

The Joyful Child Foundation program is dedicated to preventing crimes against children through programs that educate, empower and unite families and communities. The Brave program teaches kids 5-17 how to be safe. Erin Runnion started the foundation in the memory of her daughter. Samantha was only 5 years old when she was kidnapped, raped and cruelly murdered. Erin is a true heroine in the fight for kids and one of the most inspiring people you will ever meet. *(9.4)*

Teachers and youth pastors can use all these resources and make the program more meaningful to their group of kids by incorporating information that the "Netsmartz," "iGuardian" and "Enough is Enough" videos address. An all-time great handout that educators can use is at www.sowerseducation.com. Under the Resources tab, select "Handout, Pimp Tactics...." This handout provides a reference for the tactics of the "Gorilla," "Romeo" and "CEO Pimp." If the school is in a gang area, then a section on how to avoid gang recruitment is critical. Tailor making a program might necessitate meeting with local police, Social Services, etc. It is important to do this because if kids continue to think that Human Trafficking is an issue that is mainly happening in foreign countries, their guard will be down.

To find the "Netsmartz", videos, go to the site for "The National Center for Missing and Exploited Children" and select "Teens" at the top and on the right "Real Stories, Real Impact." Recommended are "Julies Journey," "Survivor Stories," and "Amy's Choices." These videos deal with cyber exploitation and depict teens telling their own true stories about having been solicited online. They speak directly to where a teen lives. Julie shares about how her online "boyfriend" was texting her over 20 times a day. She felt that he was the only one in the world who truly understood her. When she finally met him and discovered that he was a man over 40, she did not care because he made her feel truly loved. At the end she shares how it was all a lie, how she had been used. It is a very effective video.

But let's not forget that boys are victims too, which is why it is also important to show "Survivor Stories." Even if a teen is not being solicited online for sex, this video wakes boys up to the fact that there are "strangers" out there who know how to act sympathetic, understanding, etc. in order to seduce teen boys into the world of Trafficking or partnering with them in committing crimes. It is important to show both sexes both videos because it is often the boys who will warn their female teen friends about the "Romeo" pimp, while the BFF girlfriend may be sucked into her friend's stories about all the gifts and attention she is getting and think it is romantic. Men/boys oftentimes have an easier time seeing through the intentions of other men.

Teachers and Youth Pastors need to talk about pornography and its usage. A great website for anyone of Faith is www.pureintimacy.org. Given that this site is a conservative Christian site you might not agree with their information on homosexuality, but you can use the information for Ministry Leaders as a guide for how to work with teens who might find themselves involved in pornography. Ministry Leaders can promote the awesome program that "Fight the New Drug" has for teen porn addicts entitled "Fortify." They can utilize the resources at this site and ask this group to come and present their talk entitled "Porn Kills Love."

Youth need to stay active. They get bored easily and will tolerate only so much education before you need to find social activities for them to keep them involved. One activity that will really change their heart is to have them offer to "kid sit" foster kids at Foster care organizations. These agencies often offer continuing education for their foster parents

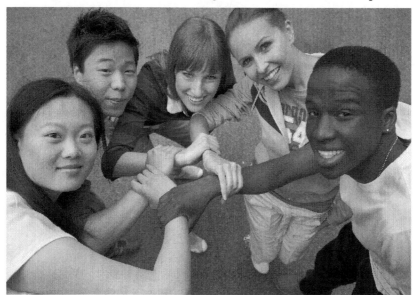

Given that this crime is aimed at youth, it is important to get them involved.

and provide child care while they attend the class. The foster children are supervised by a social worker and they need teens there to help play with the kids. The most common response I have heard from people who have "kid sat" is that these kids seem so normal. Foster Kids often will seem like "normal" kids who are exceptionally wired as kids with anxiety will often come across as being "wired." This is one way to inspire our future generations to become foster and adoptive parents and mentors. There are very, very few opportunities for kids under 18 to come in contact with foster kids and this is one of them.

Creative teens like to make posters. They can make some to put up at schools, warning other teens about the ways kids are solicited. The Traffickers have recruited teenage pimps and taught them how to seduce teens by flattering them, buying them presents and the like. Teens can make up posters to warn other teens of how the "Romeo Pimp" operates. I would love to see Facebook posts from teens, something to the effect....."It doesn't matter how much he says he loves you, if he wants you to run away with him or have sex with a stranger, he is a Pimp and he is using you." Parents might find that a little too blunt but anyone who hangs around teens know that teens are very, very "straight" with each other and don't respond well to subtlety. Somehow we need to break through the stupor a lovesick teen is in and if it takes shock to do that, then we need to do what is necessary to protect them.

Social media posts warning teens how female "teen pimps" get their friends involved is another idea for a post or poster. The post can say something like "Sure the money is good, until you get AIDS or beaten to death." Keep in mind that 12 and 13 year old junior high kids are a main target for Traffickers because 12 year olds are easily manipulated. Also "Clients" are afraid of AIDS and they think that the younger the kid, the less likely they will get an STD which puts Junior High kids in high demand. Also these kids can be marketed as virgins which justifies a very high price. So we need to start warning kids at the 5th grade level.

The teens can also create posters warning homeless teens and young adults how Traffickers trick them. These posters can be put up at bus and train stations, food courts at malls and all the other places that "at risk" teens may hang out. Teens can also do skits at school assemblies to raise awareness regarding the ploys Human Traffickers use to recruit teens.

Live2free.org is a great site to get ideas for activities that teens can do to raise awareness and participate in the community. One of their activities is to go to malls and do a "Freeze" skit where they freeze in different positions, holding up their posters. One project they did was to go to health clinics and pass out information to Health Care providers in Orange County, California. Within a week, 2 victims were rescued as a result of their efforts. *(9.5)* This group is made up of college kids who make presentations at High Schools to raise awareness and educate teens what actions they can take. Their interactive presentation is awesome and something you can request for your youth group if you are located in Southern California. If not, you can ask them if they can share their presentation with you.

Many campaigns to educate and raise awareness with teens are brilliant. Rochester, New York is making public service announcement to let youth know where they can get help. *(9.6)* The Crisis Center of Tampa Bay and the Florida Coalition Against Human Trafficking launched a campaign dubbed "Drop an F-Bomb," which is designed to grab the attention of teens through social media. This is a great example of organizations collaborating to raise awareness among naive teens. "F" stands for "Friend" and the campaign lets teens know that there is someone they can talk to if they think they themselves or a friend are in danger from a Trafficker/Recruiter. *(9.7)*

Another great program is through www.caase.org, the "Chicago Alliance Against Sexual Exploitation." In their blog, one of the staff shares about a program he did with 9th grade boys. He asked them what they called prostitutes. Then he asked them if they referred to the other girls at school the same way. They were and by doing that, the staff member had them see that they were conditioning the women they know to be receptive to becoming prostitutes. Many groups have recognized that boys/men's attitude towards woman is creating demand and making woman more vulnerable to becoming trafficking victims. Crittenton is coming out with a program at the beginning of 2015 that addresses boy's attitudes towards women.

In the "Ending Human Trafficking" podcast #62, Jonathon Walton was interviewed. Jonathon is InterVarsity's Christian Fellowship Urban Project Director. This fellowship is the largest student group in the world and Jonathon represents them as one of "New York's New Abolitionists." Jonathon shared that 95% of kids who reach NYC meet a pimp within their first 24 hours and that 65% will engage in some sort of sex act to survive. The Christian Fellowship and New York Urban Projects raises awareness among college kids as to the many activities they can do in their own city for justice. You can contact them for ideas.

The International Justice Mission has lots of great information, including inspiring videos of kids from age 10 on up who are making a difference in raising awareness regarding Human Trafficking. They also offer a conference for college kids and many other activities that teens can do. (www.ijm.org) Another great way to get the youth involved is to have teens read books by Zach Hunter, the teen abolitionist. He truly speaks their language. He has a toolkit at his site to start a "Loose Change 2 Loosen Chains" campaign, together with T-shirts and other materials. This campaign is a great way to raise awareness with teens by having them actively engage in doing a project to fight Trafficking in developing countries. Click on "loosechange2loosenchains," at the top of his site. (www.zachhunter.me) Following is a post from Zach's site:

"YOU ARE THE SOMEONE. TODAY IS THE DAY. You don't have to look very far to know that our world is a messed up place. People are hurting. Suffering is everywhere. It can be really overwhelming. You might wonder why someone isn't doing something. Where is the help? Or you may think that if you're going to make a difference, it will be someday ... when you're older, better educated, have more money, or have fewer problems of your own. Well, this morning when you woke up, there were people around the world and in your own community who were hoping that today might be the day. The day someone stepped in between slaves and their oppressors. The day relief from suffering begins. The day they could feed, clothe and educate their kids.

The day someone showed kindness to them, or let them know they had value. Please, know this -- while you may not be able to do everything -- and you can't solve all of the problems alone- working together, our generation CAN make a difference. Don't wait for someone else. Don't wait for someday because YOU are the someone and TODAY is the day"

References: (9.1) Physicians News Digest, "Doctors Should Have Formal Education on Human Trafficking" 7.21.14 Brad Broker
(9.2) Agent for Homeland Security
(9.3) Example provided by a Los Angeles Social Worker.
(9.4) Erin Runnion, speaker at CottonWood, Reset Event, 1.21.14.
(9.5) Conversation with Sandra Morgan, Vanguard University
(9.6) WHEC NEWS "Safe Harbour Program launches new videos to raise awareness of human trafficking" by Nikki Rudd
(9.7) The Tampa Tribune. 6.9.14 "'Drop an F-Bomb' campaign targets human trafficking." By Keith Morelli

CHAPTER TEN

The Key to Ending Trafficking is to Start a Group

y main goal when I speak is to set up a church ministry. It often takes the form of engaging a men's group or a women's group or the Social Justice Committee, etc. to do 2 or 3 activities a year to educate people on what they can do. If we are going to end Trafficking, we need to engage groups to take on the fight for years. Otherwise all we have are people reading an article from time to time or listening to a news story and stressing about how terrible it all is and then going on with their life. We need to keep this issue in front of people so they stay motivated to protect adults and kids from becoming used by the greed of others. The suggestions in this chapter could be utilized by any type of group, including Service Clubs like The Jr. League, Soroptomists, etc.

These ministries or groups have two purposes. One purpose is to do an activity together at their place of worship or as a club, which will bind the group together, something meaningful and social that they can do that inspires action within their community. In this chapter we will focus on activities that can be easily done where people worship. The second purpose would be to support individual members in whatever project they are doing in the community. You can suggest people in

Places of worship are ideal places to start a group.

your ministry/group read this book or share at your meetings what is in this book for ideas on what to do.

While one is limited as to what they can do at a place of worship, there is no limit as to the amount of awareness you can raise in your community as suggested throughout the book. For instance the nurses in the group can meet separately over lunch and download the materials suggested in the chapter for health professionals and make an effort to get the nurses in their community trained. They would then report to the group how they are doing and the group could cheer them on. Someone in your group could be a teacher who wants to raise awareness with his/her students or they might be another Kendis Perris who raised awareness in the trucking industry or another Rachel Lloyd who does street outreach, or another Annie Lobert who started "Hookers for Jesus." Members of the group could go to the city and make an argument to create shelters for kids where the group can volunteer or encourage the city to close down massage parlors where solicitation is taking place. Everyone needs encouragement to keep going and this group can provide that.

Organizing a group can be done through "Meet Ups," Parent Groups,

Service Clubs, etc., and through places of worship. The advantage of starting a group at a place of worship or having a Service Club do an activity is that the infrastructure is already in place. Churches already do donut sales, it is just a matter of scheduling your group to do one, one Sunday and pass out flyers. Churches and Service Clubs already do drives, it is just a matter of finding an organization you want to support and finding out what they need.

If you approach your pastor with "*we* need to do something about this," what that pastor hears is that you expect he/she to do something and they are often not very receptive because of how busy they are. I have listened to people tell me that their pastor wasn't interested in supporting a particular project they had in mind only to find out they used the "we" approach. Pastors became pastors because they are compassionate individuals who want to serve the community, but they can only do that with teams of people who are willing to organize themselves to act.

A better approach is to let the pastor know that you have a group that wants to create a ministry to raise awareness regarding what people can do to fight Human Trafficking and you only need a few minutes to meet with them to go over the details. You will often be passed off to a deacon or church administrator which is okay. All you will ask for at that meeting is a room to meet from time to time and a few Sundays a year to have a simple event like a drive. Your group could start small, with just your prayer group and when you do a drive, etc., you can recruit people who come up to your table to join your ministry/group. It usually does not work to ask for a fundraiser at first as many faith communities need funds themselves. However, a speaker can ask for corporate sponsors which simply means requesting that people go to the management of the company they work for and ask them if they will include an organization as part of their corporate giving.

You can always invite speakers. Anyone from a foster care agency, a mentoring agency, prison ministry, the local police to educate the community on how to be safe. You could do a screening for a movie like "In Plain Sight" and have a "movie night" and provide child care as this is not a subject parents want their children exposed to.

There are lots of "drives" that you can do. Organizations that are taking care of teens need interview suits, bicycles, backpacks, etc. Covenant House needs blankets as they give out 500 blankets a month during the winter at many of their locations. You could do a "Freedom Bag" drive. Members of the faith community or service organization bring backpacks and personal items, socks, t-shirts, sweatpants, etc. These bags are for rescued victims as the victims often come into a rehabilitation program with only the clothes they are wearing, nothing else.

Many organizations like "Stand Up for Kids" need shoes for homeless kids or cell phones so their youth can get a job. A good time to do this drive is right after Christmas when many people get new phones and are looking to get rid of their old phones. You just need to get the bulletin announcement scheduled for your drive and ask for a 30 second announcement the week before at the end of the service. Then come next week and set up your table.

Any type of activity, including fundraisers that will make "at risk" kids "visible" will make a difference. Sponsoring a Christmas party or taking a group of foster kids on an outing, like to a baseball game, is very effective as a foster/adoptive parent recruitment activity, because once people meet the kids their fears are put to rest and their heart goes out to them. For any activity that you do, in the bulletin announcement and at your table, you can provide information as to why your drive or activity is part of the fight to end Trafficking.

Most ministries are limited by how much they can do at a church as there are other competing ministries that also want do to activities. A "White Ribbon" campaign, a drive, a "Fair Trade" and/or "Foster/Mentoring" awareness event, may be all that your group can do in one year. Advertisers will tell you that four activities a year are enough, if done every year. No matter what theme your group chooses for the drive that you do, the point of these activities is to have flyers at your table educating people on all aspects of how they can make a difference in the fight against Trafficking. You can include flyers that educate people about the connection between "Fair Trade" and labor trafficking and/or how foster kids are vulnerable to becoming trafficked and on that flyer include information on foster care orientations that people can go to, to get more information. Always have a flyer that educates people as to what "Human Trafficking looks like" with the 888 number.

The staff at every organization I have talked to will tell you that it takes anywhere from 4 to 10 contacts with a person before they will commit to be a mentor, a foster parent or a volunteer for their organization. It is not that they don't want to do it, they do. But given human nature being what it is, they need to be invited more than once before they will commit.

Groups can also raise awareness on how to reduce child abuse which is a root cause for why many kids run away and wind up as Trafficking victims. You could have classes for parents on how to discipline their children. One of my best experiences at being a foster/adoptive mom was the opportunity to take all the parenting classes. My favorite was "1,2,3 Magic." ($15 to purchase, ages 5 – 12) Essentially what you do is sit down with your children and tell them that the reason why you yell is because they have trained you to do that, because they don't act unless you start yelling. So instead you are going to stop yelling and when they misbehave, you say "That's One." If you reach 3, then the consequences are enacted.

Social Services usually partners with an agency that provides programs to help parents avoid child abuse and those organizations have flyers letting people know where they can get help. The most likely person to abuse a child is a single mother around three in the afternoon when her blood sugar is low. Just making people aware that when you feel that you can't handle listening to your baby scream another minute would be a good time to put that child in a playpen and walk outside for a couple of minutes, could save many children from abuse.

If the result of all this is that your group enrolled people into purchasing "Fair Trade," recruited a dozen mentors and a couple of volunteers who talked a kid out of running away and/or created a handful of new foster and adoptive parents and woke your church up to the dangers of pornography and provided a foster care organization with backpacks, you would have changed the lives of dozens of kids and all who they touch forever! It would also transform the lives of all those who volunteer. You could even have fun doing it!

It is important for those of us who are leaders not to assume that another's calling is the same as yours. We need to honor what God has put on everyone's heart. I speak at churches at the end of the service and have a table outside so people can talk to me about what they can do. I had someone come up to my table who really wanted to do street outreach and go find kids on the beaches, etc., and talk to them. I recommended he contact "Stand up for Kids." This is not something that appeals to me personally because connecting with teens is not my gift. However, it is not my job to only enroll people in what I like.

My job and yours is to help people discover what gifts they have and to empower them in what God has called them to do. In talking to him further he shared with me that he had once been homeless and overcame it and passionately wanted to help others to do the same. He had been looking for an organization to volunteer for and was thrilled that I knew of one where he could use his unique experience to contribute.

In another instance, an elderly woman came up to me and told me she wanted to do something but felt she was too old to take on any of the actions I had mentioned in my talk and started walking away. I asked her to wait and we talked about what community she was part of and I suggested she do a blanket drive. So she put flyers up in her retirement community, recruited other seniors to help her and collected 500 blankets for Covenant House and now she is "on fire." Her group is now going out to stores to collect "about to be expired" peanut butter and bread so they can donate it to organizations like Covenant House where they feed a lot of people. Her senior group proudly shares how they are fighting Human Trafficking. It empowers people when you facilitate them to take action.

I used to be hesitant to tell people what to do but without someone taking the lead, groups tend to fall apart. What I have found works best is to start with a couple of simple projects like a donut sale or a drive to get the group to start working together. If at the beginning you spend too many meetings trying to plan a big activity, the members will lose interest and your group might fall apart. When you start your group you should have an activity planned by the second meeting. Later, when your group has solidified, you can take on bigger projects. In the beginning you should meet often, then you should meet at least once a month. Members can bring their ideas of what to do to the meeting or share what they just read about or what they heard other people are doing to fight Trafficking.

Members can report on a local organization that they met with. They would report on the purpose of the organization, who it serves and the needs of that organization. The group can then discuss ways they could support that organization. I always invite my groups to attend local orientations for organizations that are rehabilitating victims or helping kids, so that they can learn from those who have had first-hand experience working with "at risk" teens and victims. In other words, they can go to a CASA orientation or one for the foster care system so when people come up to the tables at your drive, the volunteers will be knowledgeable and can answer questions. They can speak from personal experience about what local organizations are doing, which is always more effective in getting people to participate, than quoting something from the internet.

So start your meetings with a prayer, read a relevant scripture, have fun and focus the conversation as to what actions you are going to take. It is very seductive to talk about the suffering of the victims and how the government or some other entity needs to do more or how evil the Traffickers are. You need to manage that type of conversation so it only takes up 15% of your meeting time or you will end your meeting with no actions being planned. While people do need to vent, as leaders you always want to look at the result you produced and you don't want the only result to have been a meeting that was a only a venting session for your members. Your meetings need to be a place where the group plans specific actions to end trafficking in your community.

CHAPTER ELEVEN

Lets' Raise Money and Have Fun Doing It!

All the organizations that are working on this issue such as "Not For Sale," "Free the Slaves" and the ones taking care of kids like "Covenant House," "Stand up for Kids," "CASA," etc. as well as the organizations that rehabilitate victims, like the Salvation Army, all need money. In Third World countries, pastors will sometimes keep the rescued kids in the church basements and they often go without eating for days. The Traffickers know the kids are there and go to those churches to find them. At great risk to themselves, the people at the church tell the Traffickers "You can't have this one!" If you would like to contribute to a foreign effort the best place to find them is through mission groups from your local faith community. This crime is so widespread that most mission groups know of a rescue effort in the Third World countries they serve. You can always contact the International Justice Mission or Free the Slaves to find out how you can support foreign efforts.

If you are a member of an NGO that is fighting Trafficking, we offer strategies for raising money that is working, that we won't cover here as this book is targeted towards what individuals can do. If you would like to learn more, please email us at ucanfightht@throughGodsgrace.com.

You can donate to organizations that provide Micro Financing which has a powerful impact on protecting "at risk" families in the Third World. If you are not familiar with micro financing, at the World Vision website are stories about families who have been helped through micro-financing and how whole communities have been able to escape the cycle of poverty through these short term loans which you can raise money for. One of the many worthwhile things I have done in life is to participate in the "Just Faith" program whose purpose is to inspire one to act for justice, through stories of people like you and me who have made a difference. One story was of a Mexican apple farmer who was planning on coming to the U.S. illegally because he could no longer afford to feed his children. His apple farm was not making the profits he needed to provide for his family and his workers were in the same position, so the entire village was planning on leaving. He didn't want to come to the U.S and leave his children behind but he didn't see any other option.

Catholic Relief Services approached him and gave him a micro-finance loan and taught him a marketing plan to increase his profits. First they showed him how to prune his apple trees so the apples got really big. Then they had the farmer put his apples in an oxygenated environment which preserved them so he could sell the apples as gourmet apples in the winter, instead of the small ones in the Spring. He did so well that he paid back the loan in less than a year and employed several families in his village which made it possible for them to stay in Mexico, rather than coming to the U.S. illegally. Supporting organization that are providing micro-finance loans is a way to reduce trafficking as it makes families stronger by enabling mothers and fathers to stay in their own countries and protect their children.

Raising money can be fun. You could go to the Polaris Project and under "Take Action" you could invite your friends or co-workers to take on some of their ideas under "Fundraise." People love participating in social or competitive events. One activity your group could do would be to host a competitive bicycle race with prizes and a spaghetti dinner afterwards. Churches that have done this have raised thousands. You could contact Oxfam or Heifer International and find out how much money it would take to buy ten goats for a village and make that your faith community or your service group's goal. Then you could put a picture of a goat on your banner with the goal which makes your project more meaningful. You just need to use your imagination as to the many types of fundraising you can do. Here are some other ideas:

You could have a jewelry party which supports organizations like Destiny Rescue who rescues child victims in Asia. Also, women will often host Candle, Mary Kay, etc. parties as an excuse to socialize. Hostesses get a percent of the sales in the form of products for hosting the party. Instead of getting candles or pots, hostesses can get cash and donate it. You could have an annual Candle, etc. party for a worthwhile organization, have wine and snacks, socialize and raise awareness.

Recycle Drives, Plant Sales, Bake Sales, etc. can all be done at your place of worship. You want to make sure you have a donation jar, even at a recycle drive so people know they can write checks. You just need a bulletin announcement and for the person leading the service to take a minute to invite people to go buy a plant, etc. and share how what you are doing is helping kids and protecting them from being trafficked or that the money will be used to help victims.

You can Google "Blood for Missions" and learn how to raise money by doing a blood drive. Or do a "Car Wash" for a day and donate the proceeds. You can always donate a car, boat etc. to an organization that will sell it and give the proceeds to your favorite charity.

There are always Personal Cocktail Parties you can do as fundraisers. You can invite your friends to donate their talents like comedy or singing for your party. People like to dress up, socialize and have fun. Most organizations like CASA, Covenant House, etc. have an annual fundraiser. Invite your friends to go with you and have fun!

You can participate in the Covenant House "sleep out" which is a fundraiser. Think of the people you will meet who are willing to sleep on the ground with you in solidarity with homeless youth! Do you like to run, swim, ride, etc.? Then participate in a local 10K to raise money and awareness. One Real Estate agent enrolled the agents in his office to

You will meet awesome people if you choose to participate in a "sleep out."

run in a marathon to raise money for a local rehabilitation home. How about those of you who are climbers? Ben Wicks and Rob Garey founded "Climb for Captives" a mountain climbing fund raising group. Their message is "Use what you love to do to end what you hate." *(11.1)* The "Not for Sale Campaign" has a "Free to Play" campaign where anyone at any age, can donate as part of the game. The program began when the son of David Batstone, founder of "Not for Sale," got his six grade basketball team to donate 10 cents for each basket they made. There are many creative and fun activities where you could get your friends, school or entire office involved.

You can also go to www.covenanthouse.org and select "Get Involved" at the top and scroll down to "Home Team." Covenant House offers guaranteed entrance for some of the country's premiere endurance events such as the Walt Disney World Marathon Weekend, TCS NYC Marathon, Philadelphia Marathon, NYC Half Marathon, NYC! Triathlon, and the TD Five Boro. Many organizations have athletic events you can participate in. Think of how much fun you will have!

You can host a screening event like the one that is being done with the movie "Girl Rising." (www.girlrising.com) This film illustrates how educating girls is one of the most powerful ways to fight Trafficking in the developing world. It supports strong families and also increases the GNP of those nations, making them stronger and less vulnerable to any type of crime. Top economists have estimated that it will cost 28 billion to provide education for every child in the world which is the amount that the charities in the state of Michigan spent in a year. *(11.2)* To reiterate the theme of Chapter Two, we have the resources, what is missing is the political will to make it happen.

Parents are always looking to take a break from their children. You could host a movie night for kids with volunteers from your church who will "kid-sit" and charge @$10 or more for the evening. I promise you, this will be a popular event! Even better, have someone there who has been "vetted" by the foster care system and is authorized to watch foster kids and make this a "no charge" event for foster parents as a way to support them and raise awareness for the need for foster parents.

You can always feed people. See if your local store will donate the food. Make it fun. Host a "Casino Night," or host a dance, a talent show, a karaoke competition, an obstacle course competition or a hula hoop contest. People can vote and cheer for their friends. Any kind of luncheon will also work, especially if you offer entertainment like a Fashion Show or Magic Show.

One church donated the proceeds from their "Lenten Fish Fry" to an organization that took care of street kids. The awareness raising is as important as the money raised because it makes those vulnerable to becoming victims of this crime "visible." Having a theme for an activity that your church does every year anyway like a "Lenten Fish Fry," makes raising money and awareness simple and easy.

In the book "Justice Awakening," Eddie Bynum shared that during lent his church fasted by giving up one meal a day and donated the money they would have spent for that meal. Their "Fast for Freedom" project raised $75,000.

Do a rummage sale. My church did one and we told people they could only donate "good stuff" like designer clothes they no longer wanted, computers, video game systems, etc. It was a huge success.

Hair salons can do a hair cutting day where a percent of the money is donated. You could invite people in different professions like handymen to donate their services for a limited number of calls. Who in your faith community has a service they can donate? You could raffle it off.

An Elks Club in Western Kentucky got really creative. They hosted a "Whiskers and Chrome" event. The event featured a motorcycle show and best beard competition to benefit a local organization that raises awareness and helps victims. The participants had a blast. *(11.3)*

Corporate Giving- You can ask your company to contribute to Micro financing to help people in the Third World or include some of the organizations at the "Freedom Registry" or "Engage Together" as part of their corporate giving. Corporations would be smart to contact an organization like "Stand Up for Kids" and provide the monies for them to do a show on the plight of street kids with your company named as the sponsor. Human Trafficking is a popular topic and it would do well for your corporate image to be associated with fighting for kids.

A note here, Human Trafficking is a hot topic and many new organizations are springing up that need money, but they don't have the experience or infrastructure to fulfill on their mission. New groups really need to get trained by established organizations that have been doing similar work for years. Also where there is public compassion, there are scams. Groups are purchasing 501C certifications from charities that are going out of business, so they can claim that they have been in business for many years, when really they just established themselves. Whenever an organization is asking for money you need to do some research before you recommend them to your faith community or organization. The groups mentioned in this book are all well established with strong track records for helping kids and victims of Human Trafficking.

References: (11.1) Kirkland Reporter. "Kirkland man helps start climbing group to end slavery." Sarah Kehoe 8.30.14 www.climbforcaptives.com
(11.2) "Ending Slavery" by Kevin Bales, page 35.
(11.3) The Winchester Sun. "Whiskers and Chrome raises funds for human trafficking awareness." Whitney Leggett 8.26.14

CHAPTER TWELVE

LAWS

"In recent years we've pursued a comprehensive approach reflected by the three Ps: prosecution, protection, and prevention. Well, it's time to add a fourth: partnership. The criminal network that enslaves millions of people crosses borders and spans continents. So our response must do the same. So we're committed to building new partnerships with governments and NGOs around the world, because the repercussions of trafficking affect us all." Secretary of State Hillary Rodham Clinton, June 16, 2009.

To date, hundreds of countries have joined the coalition to strengthen their laws against Trafficking. For that reason you will find similar laws in many countries. The TIP Report, which can be found at the U.S. Department of State website, outlines efforts on behalf of government around the world. Kevin Bales emphasizes in his book "Ending Slavery, How We Free Today's Slaves," that government participation is critical to ending slavery. He cites the 2006 example of the U.S. armed forces banning soldiers from patronizing brothels. The brothels had been set up almost exclusively for military use. His book highlights the need to end police corruption in the developing world and suggests that we make fighting trafficking, one of the jobs of the UN peacekeeping troops. The police are often paid by the Trafficker to look the other way which is why the International Justice Mission is in the Third World. IJM provides an incorruptible legal team to help the NGO's who are rescuing victims, convict the Traffickers.

This chapter only focuses on laws in the U.S. that may or may not exist outside of the U.S. However, no matter where you live, you will find this information useful as it gives you an idea of what can be accomplished through regulation. In addition to actively working to create stronger laws against trafficking, in every country you research you will find that they are also doing a lot of prevention training. In the U.S., Homeland Security is training taxi cab drivers, bus drivers, the coast guard, postmen mail carriers, airline personnel, etc. as to what to look for and what actions to take. *(12.1)* You need to ask these entities where you live if they have done this training.

Laws are only effective if they can be enforced and for that reason law enforcement tells us that they need community partnership to make the end of Trafficking a reality because they can't be everywhere. The purpose of this chapter is to provide enough education so the average person knows when to call the police. Legal websites tend to state laws in a way that only an attorney or police officer can understand it, so this chapter has been simplified. It is not designed to train law enforcement

Citizens need to continue to encourage government to act.

or attorneys. Both these groups need to seek out workshops or websites within their field so they can be empowered to act.

If you see a child under 18 being sold for prostitution or if you come across incidents of labor Trafficking, you should call the police. You are welcome to call the police if you see an individual involved in prostitution who is over 18, but given it is a misdemeanor your call may be given a low priority. If you run across someone explicitly selling a child online, call the Human Trafficking hotline – 1-888-3737-888.

Twenty five years ago my husband and I leased an executive suite for our business and there was a businessman there named Tom. I said "Hi" to Tom (not his real name) every day and would sometimes sit in his office to "chat" while in between clients. One day he told me he was going on vacation and I asked him where and he said "Thailand." So I asked him why he was going to Thailand. He smiled and with complete sincerity said "Thailand has a very different culture than we do. They are not uptight about sex like we are. From the time children are young, they are taught to enjoy sex and I am going over there to see what it is like to have sex with the children there."

I found that very disturbing but accepted his matter of fact explanation that in this foreign country, because of their mindset children were not being abused. (I was naive!) I rationalized it because I knew Tom and he was a really nice guy, someone a friend of mine had dated. What often blocks our ability to recognize what is going on is the assumption that a trafficker, sex addict or a pedophile will never be someone you personally know. We assume that pedophiles and criminals are monsters, easily recognizable. That was one of the reasons neighbors on the street in Ohio where three women were imprisoned for years, weren't suspicious. Ariel Castro was very charming.

The kind of "vacation" Tom was describing is referred to as a "sex tour" and you can find them all over the internet if you know where to look. Tom's rationalization was one he got from a child porn website and he clearly did not think he was doing anything wrong. He wasn't breaking any laws (at the time) because he wasn't having sex with children in the U.S. and according to the brainwashing he had gotten from the child porn websites, the children enjoyed the sex and sex with children was OK in the country where he was going, so what was the harm?! In addition the sites promoted how great the sex was so it sounded like a great vacation.

If I were to have that conversation today, I would have told Tom that he had been lied to, that those children had been sold by their poor families so the youngest could eat. I would have told him that for an adult to have sex with a child, it is extremely painful, a form of torture. Despite the injury, these children will never be taken to a doctor. They will be forced to continue to have sex with men over and over again. They live in excruciating pain and extreme fear. Given how many STD's they are exposed to, combined with poor nutrition, their lives are short.

The website www.fightslaverynow.org relates the following.... It wasn't until 2003 that the U.S. passed the "Protect Act," a law that makes it illegal for American citizens to go on these "tours." However, only 5 states, Alaska, Hawaii, Missouri, New York and Washington, currently have laws that prohibit the operation of these businesses. These businesses promise 'exotic vacations for men'." (You will need to check with your state to find out if they have laws prohibiting sex tours as this post is not current.) While the businesses that provide these tours do post warnings that having sex with a child under 18 is against the law, these tours are putting "tourists" in touch with pimps who will provide whatever they desire, once they arrive at their destination.

American citizens make up 25% of the total sex tourism industry. *(12.2)* If Tom were to have shared with me about his "vacation" today, I would have threatened to report him if he went. If you suspect that someone is going on a sex tour, you can go to the DOJ website and search for "Trafficking in Persons and Worker Exploitation" for tips on what to do and there is a hotline 888-428-7581. The DOJ site has the laws for sex tourism.

I am asked all the time, "Is it a felony or misdemeanor to have sex with a prostitute?" so I asked a member of the Human Trafficking Task Force in California. It is a misdemeanor to solicit/engage in sex with a prostitute in California if she is over 18. It is also a misdemeanor for the prostitute. If the prostitute is underage, she technically should not be charged for prostitution because it is considered human trafficking and she is viewed as a victim. If a "john" or client solicits sex from someone who is underage, it's still a misdemeanor but it is possible to charge the "client" with a felony if there was evidence to support that he knew the prostitute was underage.

In California, Proposition 35 was passed which increased penalties and amended the current law on Trafficking, so that anyone who causes, induces or persuades a person under the age of 18 to engage in commercial sex is committing a crime. The minor does not even have to be involved in the sex act. The law only applies for the purpose of commercial sex. Non-commercial sex acts involving a minor is considered statutory rape, but the age of the boyfriend is taken into consideration such as two teens having consensual sex, which might not be considered rape. As for soliciting minors for commercial sex from chat rooms, the solicitation in itself is a crime.

The good news is that with increased awareness among law enforcement, more and more often the prostitute is being looked at as a victim. Police are being educated to know what to look for. What they may see is a young girl who is very savvy about sex, who portrays her pimp as a good guy and who may even be coming on to the officer sexually. They may even cuss out the police who are trying to help them. In the past, it was easy to see that girl as a "bad girl" prostitute. Police have now been trained to see those same actions as an example of a girl who is confused, as a result of having been brainwashed by her pimp.

Recently in California, upon making a routine traffic stop a policeman noticed a young teen dressed provocatively in the back seat, who did not look like the daughter of the couple in the front seat. So he asked the girl to get out of the car so he could talk to her privately. This action resulted in the couple being arrested for Human Trafficking. This is an example of an arrest having been made as the result of training the police regarding what they need to be looking for.

While gangs and criminal organizations tend to be involved in sex trafficking, white collar workers like real estate agents, college profess-sors, etc. have often been found to be involved in labor trafficking that may involve domestic servants, elder care facilities, nail salons, etc. The 2012/2013 "The State of Human Trafficking in California" report includes many examples of how victims are tricked with promises of jobs and how they are treated once they get here. The Polaris Project often has legislative action items regarding trafficking and as of the publication date of this book, their site is advocating for "H.R. 3344, the Fraudulent Overseas Recruitment and Trafficking Elimination Act of 2013" which would ensure: 1.No more lying in contracts. 2. No more fees. 3. More oversight of recruiters. We need to advocate for laws like this one in every country that does not have laws that protect victims of labor trafficking.

California recently implemented Senate Bill 1193, adding Section 52.6 to the Civil Code which mandates that certain businesses post information about human trafficking. At the California Department of Justice site, you can search for "model notice" and find this specific statement that is required for the postings: "If you or someone you know is being forced to engage in any activity and cannot leave -- whether it is commercial sex, housework, farm work, construction, factory, retail, or restaurant work, or any other activity -- call the National Human Trafficking Resource Center at 1-888-373-7888 or the California Coalition to Abolish Slavery and Trafficking (CAST) at 1-888-KEY-2-FRE(EDOM) or 1-888-539-2373 to access help and services. Victims of slavery and human trafficking are protected under United States and California law."

Many women who are involved in the legal commercial sex industry wind up becoming trafficked victims. We need to really crack down on employers involved in the production of porn and the commercial sex trade who are using minors. Anything that can be done that restricts a trafficker's ability to exploit another human being should be considered.

What about the "clients." Groups like Shared Hope feel that while we are becoming more aggressive at going after the Traffickers, they feel that we need to be more aggressive at going after the clients or "Johns." As a result, lawmakers are considering establishing laws that carry heavier penalties. Sweden is an example of the effectiveness of this. In the first five years after Sweden passed a law with a maximum sentence of 6 months in jail for the "client," prostitution in Sweden dropped dramatically. *(12.3)* Canada and Iceland have passed similar laws to Sweden.

There are hundreds of internet sites with articles from many major news sites like CNN and major newspapers like the L.A. Times that describe "John Schools." Apparently there is something about this model which resonates with people. "John Schools" were set up in 1995 for First Offenders by the San Francisco police department. *(12.4)* These schools have now been established across the United States, in Canada, South Korea and in the UK. While controversial as to their success, most people working on this issue feel that attending a John school is more effective than just having a "John" go to jail. What fuels the sex trade is fantasy and what the "schools" do is have former prostitutes speak on what their life was truly like. The purpose is to destroy the fantasy in the hopes that it will discourage the offenders from continuing to use prostitutes.

The offenders are given a choice of prosecution and a criminal record or paying a fine and going to the school. The savings to the city for not having to pay for the prosecution process and jail time is substantial and the fees are often used to help victims. In San Francisco, the schools operate at no cost to the taxpayers. *(12.4)* The former prostitutes share about how they used flattery to get more money and all the lies they told their "customers" such as how much they were enjoying the sex while fantasizing about torturing and killing the client. *(12.4)* They boast about robbing their clients and getting away with it as the "John" would have to admit to being involved in a crime in order to report the robbery. The women share how they were often sexually abused as children, tricked into getting into the life, severely beaten, etc. *(12.4)* By the end of the class, the men realize that the women are people, not just "whores" and that the fantasy they thought existed is not true, that the women are acting. What really touches the men is when they realize that these women could be their daughter. *(12.5)*

In order to further discourage the men the class covers STD's, a subject that most men think they know about, but really don't. *(12.4)* Many men do not know they can get an STD from oral sex. Pregnancy centers will often have a chart on a wall showing that if one were to have sex with 10 people and each of those people had sex with 10 people and each of those people had sex with 10 people, one could literally be exposed to getting an STD from thousands of people every time they have sex. With a prostitute that number goes up exponentially. Considering how many STD's one is exposed to can have a sobering effect for one who solicits prostitutes and condoms do not provide 100% protection.

These schools are for First Time Offenders only and waking up offenders to the reality of prostitution goes a long way to discourage re-offending for many. The men are also clear that the next time they are caught, it will mean jail time. Resources are offered to those who feel they may be sex addicts. However those men will often have a difficult time avoiding prostitutes in the future and may not seek help.

This is where churches and other groups can have a role in partnering with law enforcement by raising awareness of the dangers of pornography addiction and the consequences of sex addiction. Faith communities can encourage their members to get into support groups. In working with addicts you may find those that feel so far from God that picking up a bible is difficult. However they may be willing to read Harmony Dust's book "Scars and Stilettos." One man in prison who read the book, shared with Harmony that it transformed his life and he went on to start a "Recovery" group in prison for sex addicts. *(12.6)*

References: (12.1) Homeland Security Website
(12.2) www.fightslaverynow.org.
(12.3)"No to Prostitution and Trafficking," Karin Alfredson
(12.4) PBS "John Schools" 5.08.08
(12.5) CNN.com/Crime. "John Schools Try to Change Attitudes About Paid Sex."
Stephanie Chen 8.28.09
(12.6) Presentation by Harmony Dust at the Saddleback Human Trafficking
conference, 01.11.14

CHAPTER THIRTEEN

Gangs, Street Outreach and Rehabilitation

Gangs have added prostitution to drug dealing as a way to make money. According to the "State of Human Trafficking in California 2012/2013 Report," some domestic gangs have even given up traditional rivalries to partner with both other domestic gangs and transnational gangs to maximize their profits. So what can you and I do about gangs? While the police are fighting gangs on the law enforcement front, we can fight gangs on the Human front. This section outlines programs that are working to reduce gang involvement in communities.

For instance, there are kids in Juvenile Hall who may have no intention of leaving the gang when they get out but they want to make their First Communion, because everyone on some level wants to ensure their salvation. By volunteering to teach the preparation classes for communion or hosting a bible study for kids in Juvenile Hall, you are doing your part to fight the gang side of Human Trafficking. By teaching those classes you can influence a kid to turn his life around. If you are successful, you will have saved many from harm as one gang member can do a lot of damage. For men this presents an opportunity to model what it is to be a man of faith to a kid who may have had no positive male role models.

One interesting phenomenon that people who have worked in this area have shared with me is that even though gangs can be brutal, they have a fear of God. They may not be afraid of prison or even death, but they are afraid of hell, meaning they avoid killing priests or ministers. In James Martin's book, "My Life with the Saints," he shares about a priest who they called "Brother Bill." When gangs would schedule a street war, Brother Bill would go stand between the opposing gangs. He shared with Father James Martin that by getting in the middle of the fight, it allowed the gang members to walk away and still save face.

When a former gang member wants to get out, the penalty is often death. However if a gang member claims that they are leaving the gang because they turned their life over to Jesus or have become a devout Muslim, they are often left alone. The threat of death is a major concern for anyone wanting to leave the gang, but as one worker pointed out to them, if they stay in the gang they are probably going to die. In her effort to encourage them to turn their life around she tells them, "They can either die as a gang member or die trying to get out." Tough choice for a kid and they will only choose to get out if they have a community that will be there for them. Very few will make that choice if they think they will be alone.

The gangs will pick up the girls they want for sex trafficking and threaten to kill her family members if she does not cooperate. Unless that girl knows that someone can protect her family, she will feel that she has no choice. We need to create safe havens for kids so they can resist the pressure of the gangs. In the cases where the gangs have threatened to kill the family if the teen testifies, creating a "Safe Haven" may include hiding that family from the gangs in another community. We need churches to work together with Homeland Security to create a network of "Safe Havens." While Homeland Security can protect the family, the resources of law enforcement are limited. For those "at risk" families that do not qualify for "Witness Protection," faith communities can help that family relocate, get a job, secure child care, etc.

Transforming a gang community takes an effort by the entire com-

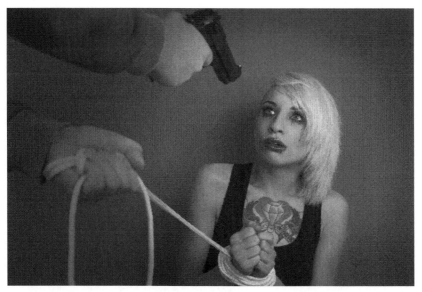

Gangs have included Human Trafficking to their list of crimes.

munity. The models that Father Gregory Boyle and Pastor Rivers created and adapted to their churches are two examples of community efforts that are working. So is the example of "SEA Charter Schools" and "Lives Worth Saving."

In his moving and inspiring book, "Tattoos of the Heart," Father Boyle shares how he became a parish priest in one of the worst gang areas in Los Angeles. Mothers came to him weeping after their sons were murdered and expressed their fears for the safety of the sons they had left. So Father Boyle talked with his parishioners until he understood that so much of gang activity in his community stemmed from the fact that even if a gang member wanted to turn his life around, it was too hard to get a job as a former gang member. So with the help of his community, Father Boyle created several businesses to employ former and current gang members who wanted out.

In addition to employment, the church offers classes to develop these young men and women into responsible individuals who can succeed in society. His T-shirts state that "Nothing Stops a Bullet Like a Job." His program has won the president's award year after year for its success in rehabilitating gang members. Like Father Boyle, we need to create employment opportunities for former juvenile delinquents and gang members that give them dignity. Given their "street smarts" they tend to do well in sales jobs. Unless we create employment opportunities for these kids, they are going to go back to what they know in order to survive.

Several years ago, at the Restorative Justice Conference that was sponsored by the Catholic Diocese of Los Angeles, Pastor Rivers was the keynote speaker. At this conference groups from all over the world were invited to share what they were doing that was working to rehabilitate youth. Pastor Rivers told his story of having been a gang member and then giving his life to Jesus. Over time, he felt called by God to serve in gang communities. So he put himself through Harvard and then the seminary to prepare himself for his mission. He became pastor of a church in one of the worst areas of Boston in order to respond to his calling to transform gang communities.

However he was very disappointed by the attendance of the youth at his church so he prayed and he prayed and one day God answered his prayer in an extraordinary way. A drug dealer came up to him and said "Pastor, I heard that you wanted to know why kids aren't coming to your church." Then the drug dealer boasted to Pastor Rivers that… "when Johnny goes to school, I am there and you are not. When Johnny comes home from school, I am there and you are not. Because I am there and you are not, I win and you lose!"

So Pastor Rivers "got it" and began a program whose theme was "Being There." He enrolled his church in establishing a youth center and becoming mentors to the teens. He convinced the Boston police to bring kids who were getting into trouble to his church, instead of juvenile hall. They turned around 9 out of 10 and gave back to the police the 10th kid they couldn't turn around. The program so drastically reduced violent crime in Boston that Pastor Rivers got National attention and variations of the program "Being There" is in dozens of communities in the U.S.

The program is administered through the "Boston Ten Point Coalition," (www.btpc.org) which is an ecumenical group of Christian clergy and lay leaders working to mobilize the community around issues affecting Black and Latino youth. Their mission "...is to end the era of violence in Boston, and demonstrate the vital need for faith-based institutions to participate in city-wide crime reduction strategy." They work in collaboration with the private sector, government and community based groups. This organization is an excellent model for any community. *(13.1)*

"Lives Worth Saving" is a model that many faith communities are taking on in collaboration with all aspects of the criminal justice system including law enforcement and the probation department. Volunteers go door to door to share about their programs and how they can help gang members leave the gangs. They believe that violence is a learned pattern and can be unlearned. They help communities achieve peace. Their program addresses domestic violence, job preparation, anger management, sports programs and many other opportunities to turn one's life around. You can read about this model for gang intervention at their site http://www.lwsgi.com.

At a Human Trafficking conference, the speaker for gangs provided the example of a four mile area in Los Angeles, where they had around 185 murders every year, year after year with "arrest and incarceration" their only approach to reducing the homicide rate. In 2000, they decided to try a "community intervention" model that included education and programs, similar to what all the examples in this chapter include. In 2014, the murder rate was 14!

"The Dream Center" is another example of setting up a community outreach that reduced crime by 73% in one of the worst crime areas in Los Angeles. They serve the community through programs that address hunger, poverty, addiction and human trafficking. Their food outreach ministry alone reaches over 50,000 people a month. There are 73 different ministries and at any one time there are 770 people "on campus" working to overcome their past and learning how to serve their community. *(13.2)*

If you think you are too old to make a contribution to your community, you would do well to consider the example of Pastor Tommy Bar-

The Dream's Center's commitment to outreach and service has transformed their community.

nett who at the age of 63 asked his church in Phoenix to sponsor his jog/walk from Phoenix to Echo Park, Ca. (375 miles) His "walk" helped raise the money to support his son Matthew to buy the abandoned Queen of Angeles hospital that now houses "The Dream Center." (13.2)

Many churches in "at risk" communities have similar outreach programs which address the needs of their community like "The Dream Center" does. If your faith community is too small to take on a community outreach activity that many of the mega churches are doing, then go volunteer with a local church so you can do your part.

SEA, which stands for Soledad Enrichment Action Inc. is a non- profit agency that is dedicated to helping high-risk youth and their families. (www.seacharter.net) It was started in 1972 by mothers whose sons had been killed as a result of gang violence. They decided to do something about it, so they met at a local church and formed a plan. They started with a school in East Los Angeles that is now a Charter school. SEA Charter Schools now has 4,000 kids at 16 different educational sites in the Los Angeles area and is the leading provider of services to high-risk individuals, families, and gang-affected communities within Southern California. *(13.3)*

The SEA schools are located in gang areas of L.A. so that kids who find themselves in danger of crossing neighborhoods can be safe and also obtain a good education. The staff at SEA understand the attraction of gangs. For many youth, the gangs provide a sense of having a cause, family, respect, mentoring, excitement, fun and the opportunity to get high on drugs. So the SEA schools duplicate those aspects of gang life by providing positive causes, respect, excitement, etc. While the school focuses on academics it also includes wrap-around services such as counseling, gang intervention, job readiness and a parenting program that aims at bringing down the violence in the family. As a result kids start to dream of a better future for themselves and their families. Gangs are not as attractive as they once were, because of new alternatives.

In addition to the tailor made curriculum, SEA has created the Youth Peace Movement (YPM) and every SEA school has a youth group of peace. These groups are given a list with the 10 global calls to action, created by the Nobel Peace Laureates. The group chooses one of the global calls and puts it into action in their neighborhood, such as feeding the homeless, cleaning the environment, alleys, planting trees, getting involved with Habitat for Humanity etc. The kids feel a sense of purpose in the service they do for their community and for others. One girl told her teacher that she was "high" after completing a service project because of the difference she had made. The teacher asked her if she was as "high" as she had been on drugs. Her response was that she was "higher" than she had been on drugs and the difference was that with drugs she didn't feel good about herself afterwards. Not only was she "high" after completing the service project she felt good about herself and wanted to do more. The activities this school makes available to the students, the wisdom in which it is administered and the way this school is structured is absolutely brilliant. *(13.3)*

In addition, the school offers 32 parenting classes a week. The parents who lead the program are former students of the previous parenting classes. The parenting program includes healing the parents of their own emotional baggage, in addition to learning new skills. These parents have to deal with suicide, homicide, violence, drugs and addiction on a scale that most families will never have to deal with. Healing and empowering the entire family is one of the many reasons why the SEA Charter School is making such a difference in gang communities. The 77% completion rate makes this one of the most successful programs out there for gang communities. *(13.3)*

If you feel called to create a similar school or already have one, it would be well worth the effort to contact this school. It would be smart for any school that is operating in a similar environment to "meet" together on a "Skype" call once a month and share what is working. I have met too many organizations that are doing great work, but doing it in a vacuum. All of them have something valuable to share with each other and while some do meet, it is often locally. What might become possible if worldwide networks were created that met monthly on a call to share what is working? The Traffickers have worldwide networks and it is their collaboration with each other that makes them so powerful. Anytime we create any type of networking to collaborate and empower each other, we become more powerful in taking on the fight.

Fighting gangs is going to take the power of a coalition of faith groups, law enforcement, local businesses and community leaders. Another model that has been championed by Senator Kristen Gillibrand is outlined in the June 16th, 2010 press release at her site. One aspect of that program is to utilize "The Jump" program which provides Federal funds to non-profits who are providing mentoring programs to "at risk" youth. Churches can consider getting involved in providing mentoring programs like Pastor Rivers did, as any model that consists of adult role modeling to "youth at risk" will have an impact.

Many faith communities are doing a mini version of what Father Gregory Boyle and Pastor Rivers created. At the very least, they are providing after school care and "walk to school" programs that has kids walking in groups with an adult, so children and teens are safe. Faith communities could set up a boxing gym at their place of worship. Young boys like to fight. They will willingly participate in being part of a boxing program. Coaches could volunteer their time and the police could patrol it so the drug dealers stay away. Boys who have learning disabilities or who are behind in school don't feel like they belong in the school environment and everyone feels the need to belong to something. Gangs provide one with a sense of belonging to a group, which is one of their biggest draws. Having a sports gym to belong to for a kid whose parents can't afford a sports program is a very powerful way to discourage gang recruitment. It always takes less effort for prevention, than it takes for rehabilitation.

Criminals who are paroled often get out and commit another crime because it is the only thing they know. One California DA shared that often people who have been busted for drugs will try trafficking because the thinking is that the only reason they were convicted is because they had drugs in their possession. They meet criminals who will boast about the money they are making and having their "girls" so under control that they will never testify against them, so it seems "smarter" to get into the business of Human Trafficking. *(13.4)* "Prison" or "Restorative Justice" type ministries address this way of thinking and support former criminals to choose a path other than crime when they get out.

Restorative Justice" groups are also creating healing projects, which communities need if they are going to move forward. A great project that was shared at the 2012 Restorative Justice conference hosted by the Catholic Diocese of Los Angeles, is one where victims go to prison and share with the convicted felon the loss and devastation their actions caused to their life. Then the prisoner is given the opportunity to share what led them to committing the crime. It may have been drug addiction. It may be because as a young boy, a pimp watched his mother "get stuff" by providing sexual favors.

None of these are justifications; it just helps the victim make some sense of what happened to them. The victim then lets the convict know that they forgive them. The convict may or may not apologize. This exercise is done for the victim in order to allow them to let go of their hate and move on which aids in their healing. For many felons, it has been an opportunity to be exposed to great love, which aids in their rehabilitation. Often, in the absence of forgiveness is revenge, which in gang communities only has the violence keep perpetuating.

The bottom line for our Faith Communities and the theme for this book is that either we will be there for kids or the Human Traffickers, the gangs, the pornographers, the drug dealers, etc., will be there for our youth. When they are there and we are not, they are winning and we are losing. The gangs have power because they are organized and loyal to each other, but there are more good citizens than there are gang members.

While there have been many heroic efforts in many gang communities, we still need more intervention in the lives of these kids. If the entire community aligned itself behind ending crime, it would end. If you feel that this is your calling, ask your local district attorney what faith communities are successfully working with gangs in your community and go learn from them and join them. It is a very empowering and energizing experience to work with like-minded people who share your passion.

Street Outreach

This section outlines various ways organizations and churches are conducting street outreach. While you have been warned to not go out to the streets and attempt to rescue prostitutes, there are faith groups that are partnering with law enforcement to rehabilitate victims of trafficking or adult prostitutes who want to "get out." By letting law enforcement know about your rehabilitation program, the police can suggest to a prostitute that they have arrested, that she/he seek shelter with you.

There are street outreach organizations that have men approach a prostitute on the street from their car as if they are soliciting her for sex, as her pimp is always watching. They can give her a card with information on a local program. The conversation needs to be less than a minute otherwise the pimp may think something more than a solicitation took place, so the men need to leave for their own safety and hers. Prostitutes are beaten severely if their pimp thinks they are contemplating leaving. Gay women rarely seek out prostitutes, so it doesn't work to have women try this approach too often.

come and go, they might not be psychologically free. So groups like "xxxchurch," "Treasures," "Hookers for Jesus," etc. rescue and rehabilitate both victims of Trafficking when they find them and individuals who are involved in the commercial sex trade.

Some well-meaning groups have gone out to "pray over" prostitutes encouraging them to "sin no more." Outreach groups need to understand that for these women, the pimp has provided food, shelter, a "family" of sorts and a way to survive. He may be the only one who ever told them that he loves them. They truly believe if they walked away, even if their pimp did not find them, they don't believe they could survive. Similar to the rehabilitation work that is done with gang members, these women feel like they will be leaving the only "family" they know and unless you are going to replace the family they came from with another one, it is doubtful your program will be successful. (13.10)

The most successful faith-based "street outreach ministries" have "Drop In" centers, where the girls/boys can wait until they can be picked up and taken out of the area. Since churches have buildings, one church partnered with the Salvation Army to provide a "Drop In" center at their church. The Salvation Army provides the services. This model could be done with many faith communities and works well. The cell phones the prostitutes have are restricted, so just offering a prostitute access to the internet, or paper and stamps to write to someone is a gift and will attract women to come take a break at your center. Prostitutes have been beaten for talking to anyone their pimp does not like so unless you can offer them a way out, it is doubtful that you will have much success if you just go out to talk to them.

One group goes to the jails to find women who have been arrested for prostitution. They talk to them at the jail and share the opportunity that their program offers. Even that has risks, as the pimps could get "wind" of that kind of effort when they come to bail their "girl" out. Any attempt to help victims should be done with an experienced, trained group in partnership with law enforcement. So if you feel this is your calling, then partner with experienced groups that are going into the sex industry to help women leave, like "Treasures" does. NGO's that the police work with that rehabilitate victims can train faith groups or can at least advise you on how to create an outreach group, how to work with the police to prosecute the Trafficker and how to be safe.

Rehabilitation

You may wonder, what happens to victims once the police pick them up. Well, if they want to go home they will be given a bus ticket. However, since many of them ran away from homes where there was abuse, they don't want to go back. So they may be dropped off at a shelter. But if their only "job skill" is hooking, they go back to what they know, unless they get into a program.

Two organizations that have been recognized for having model programs that work with victims, is Children of the Night and The Dream Center. "Children of the Night" (Chapter Six) works with former prostitutes ages 11 to 17. Keep in mind that there are many rules your program will need to follow, if you are working with minors. The Dream Center's Human Trafficking program works with victims between the ages of 18 and 59 that have been sex or labor trafficked. Their program is split into 4 phases: Rescue (72 hours), Rebuild (30 days), Restore (6 to 9 months) and Re-entry (6 months). Through this comprehensive model of services, their program impacts women both in the short-term and long-term. Immediately, women receive a safe haven, protection from their traffickers and a safety net of supportive services. Long-term, they build trusting relationships and the skills necessary to successfully cope with life after having experienced enormous trauma. *(13.11)*

During the Rescue phase, the program removes women from their trafficking circumstances. They are provided shelter and food, while being assessed for the proper longer term housing placement. The goals of the Rebuild phase are to reset victims' foundations by practicing a regular routine, obtaining personal identity documents, creating long-term and short-term goals, and making decisions about their next steps. The Restore phase focuses on developing skills (communication, conflict resolution, everyday life, etc.) through individualized care plans that may include GED and language classes, computer training, therapeutic groups, outings, church services, events, and work and art therapy.

Finally, the Re-entry phase is dedicated to career development and life planning. Residents are required to participate in Two-Wings, which provides workshops, training, and internship opportunities with the expectation of having each participant employed by its completion. Throughout the program, The Dream Center provides services that build trust and rapport so that victims feel comfortable and safe enough to testify against their traffickers. With these testimonies, law enforcement is able to make convictions, helping to break the rampant cycle of abuse in the city and state. *(13.11)*

Victims have to voluntarily commit to being in any one of the programs that work with victims. Many sex trafficking victims will go back to their pimp as these programs are a lot of work and human beings tend to gravitate to what they know. The women will leave the program an average of 11 times before they stay. *(13.8)* Often the women will idealize the life they left and go back to what they know rather than stay with a program they think they will fail at. As a result of their self-esteem having been taken from them, it is very difficult for former victims to consider that they could be of value to society in any way.

For those that complete the program, they share that one of the reasons why they left is because of how deeply they had been brainwashed. The pimp will emotionally hook them by telling them that they love them. When they abuse them, it is always portrayed as the woman's fault. They don't understand that they were being abused because the pimp tells them that they were being "disciplined" for something they did. They also spiritually abuse the women. Women have been told by the pimp that God sent them to teach the girl a lesson that they were spoiled and deserved the treatment they received. *(13.12)* This results in the women being very confused as to what love and abuse really look like. Their whole view of God becomes distorted.

As a result, when the former prostitute struggles with the program and begins to idealize where they came from, they might tell the workers that their pimp loved them and the abuse was their fault. They tell themselves that when they go back, they just need to act better and the abuse will go away and all that will be left is the love that they are getting from their pimp. For those that work with these women, they will tell you that it is the hardest job they have had in working in any type of rehabilitation. These women have deep emotional, mental, spiritual and sometimes physical and drug issues, but not as many hard drugs as people think. Drugs age one and these women need to look good, so the Traffickers discourage heavy drug use. *(13.13)*

One of the many challenges the workers face is that these women have been told how to think and act for years. They lose any sense of their own identity. One of the activities in many rehabilitation programs is to take the women to a supermarket and have her pick out what she wants to eat. One victim who was in a Salvation Army program shared how incredibly difficult that was. She stood in the cereal aisle for a very long time trying to decide if she liked blueberries or chocolate and could not decide the first time she went. She had been told what to think for so long, she had lost her ability to think for herself. She stood there waiting to be told what she liked and since that did not happen, she was unable to choose. We have no concept of what it is like to have our very essence taken from us and to be as severely brainwashed as these victims are. While the rescued victims may be in a program for 2 to 3 years, in the experience of the people working with victims, it takes an average of 7 years before victims are truly restored, if ever. *(13.11)*

An additional challenge that the workers face is that the Traffickers are aware of these programs and have told a "girl" that they trust to "go get rescued," so they know where these programs are and can go get their "girls" back who have escaped. *(13.12)* These woman have lied to survive, lied to their customers, their pimp and many others. They are skilled actors and actresses, so it makes it difficult to find the ones who may be there to recruit for their pimp. Rescue workers have been threatened by the pimps. We need to pray for those who help victims.

In response to the lack of beds needed for victims, Run 2 Rescue is a rescue organization for victims of sex trafficking. Their Anchors of Hope Project will train a team to provide a home for a survivor for one year. The team will be supported by their church and with Run 2 Rescue's assistance, will provide counseling, education, and life skills guidance to the survivor for one year. Their goal is to eradicate the shortage of beds available in the United States with ONE church, helping ONE girl, in ONE home. Every "rescue and restore" group that I have talked to have emphasized how important it is for a former victim to have support in re-integrating back into the community. A faith community can invite the former victim to their Singles Group, help them get a job, help them find a sitter for their children, etc. No one does well without community support, especially those fighting depression and PTSD. Another example of an organization that works with churches to house former victims is Safe Families, with their "Safe Families Plus" program that was one of the topics as part of the In Plain Sight podcast #7. www.safe-families.org

In many cities the Salvation Army works in cooperation with the police in helping to rehabilitate victims. Groups that are doing this type of work could really use the help of faith communities and individuals to provide mentors, people to drive the victims to the doctors, help them register for school, provide shelter, jobs, help with fundraising, etc. What the former victims really need is a friend. Given the professional boundaries that staff need to employ, they can't be a friend to the wom-en they work with, but you could do that and invite them to your bible study, to go dancing, etc. So are patience and building people up two of your gifts? Then you might want to consider volunteering for those organizations that are working to rehabilitate victims. Given that only 1% of trafficking victims are ever rescued and how difficult it is to reha-bilitate victims, preventing individuals from becoming trafficked, should be a high priority for us all.

References: (13.1) From the site www.btpc.org
(13.2) From the weekly orientation that is given at The Dream Center.
(13.3) Sister Ines, Director of SEA Charter School
(13.4) Orange County, California DA
(13.5) Presentation by Children of the Night.

(13.6) Information from www.xxxchurch.com

(13.7) Information from www.iamatreasure.com

(13.8) "Hookers for Jesus" website, www.hookersforjesus.net

(13.9) Pastor Paula Daniels, presentation at Saddleback Church, Lake Forest, Ca.

(13.10) Conversation with Crittenton staff member.

(13.11) Conversation with staff member at "The Dream Center"

(13.12) Conversation with Rachel Thomas from Sowers Education.

(13.13) "Officer in Charge," Human Trafficking Unit.

CHAPTER FOURTEEN

Let's Get Started

hat I know about motivating people is that when people don't know what to do, they tend to feel lost and nothing happens. Providing ideas on what to do, is like cooking popcorn. Once you get a few ideas going, then more ideas start popping like crazy. At this point you may be overwhelmed by all the actions you want to take. So just follow your heart with regard to what God has called you to do and stay focused on one or two actions to begin with.

At the age of 16, Zach Hunter, the teenage abolitionist was on a TV show and one of the things he shared is that he felt people were too concerned with trying to discern what God has called them to do. Essentially what he said was, "God has a heart for the poor and disadvantaged so there is nothing you could possibly do to help them that would offend God, so if God has put something on your heart, you should just do it!" He inspired me to put my concerns and fears aside and just start somewhere. As often happens, the project grew. I have met scores of people who had the courage to follow their heart and go to work which inspired me to create the project I took on, which is to get out there and speak in a way that empowered individuals and faith communities to act. The goal is to encourage people to create ministries to fight Trafficking at every place of worship in the world. Creating a project and taking action can be scary if you have never done it before. But like Zach communicated, we need to "just do it!" Every day, my prayer is "God, just open the door and give me the courage to go through it."

I receive a lot of acknowledgement, which is nice and feels good but at the end of the day, what really matters is "how many mentors did I recruit? How many people did I inspire to commit to purchasing Fair Trade products? How many people did I inspire to step out with their unique gifts and take action?" I share that because in anything you take on, you need to look at what results you produced. Raising awareness is important but unless you provide a way for people to act, your awareness raising event lacked power. Having your group ask itself what results were produced, doesn't mean using that question as a way to beat yourself up or get discouraged. It means staying focused.

There are very few social issues that are not interrelated. Everyone needs to look at what is on their heart, what they are passionate about. Hopefully this book has given you some insight on how to move forward for what you believe in. For any social issue there will be actions to take in the areas of advocacy, education, ministry and prayer. Sales types tend to be drawn to advocacy, counselors to ministry/rehabilitation. We tend to be drawn to what we are good at, so while your group may feel that a particular action is really important, if you feel drawn to taking action in another area, then give yourself permission to do that.

If you are passionate about this issue and want to make a huge difference, then do the work to increase your skill set. If you are not an effective speaker then take advantage of trainings like Toastmasters. However keep in mind that it is your passion that will be powerful, not the techniques you may learn. If you want to develop your leadership skills then take advantage of the programs that Landmark offers. Your effort will fail without leadership and the ability to motivate people. Landmark Worldwide offers training in leadership and "speaking for what is possible," which motivates people to act. It includes disciplining oneself to steer away from the drama and focus on action. It also offers opportunities to break through your own personal limitations so that you can play a bigger game in life and move through obstacles with ease. For Law Enforcement and religious like priests and nuns that have taken a vow of poverty, they have a full scholarship to this program.

If you want some direction for what part you are to play in the fight, then read, "The Purpose Driven Life" by Rick Warren. If you are looking for a program that helps you discern what you have to contribute, then call the "Catherine of Siena Institute" (http://www.siena.org/) and find out when they will be doing their "Called and Gifted" workshop in your area. This is a great program to facilitate you in discerning your spiritual gifts and how to use them. The program is offered in many churches. One does not need to be a Christian to get value out of this workshop. It will be a powerful experience for anyone of any faith.

You will need to develop your prayer life so prayer is a constant in your life. This allows God to work through you. Prayer retreats are great because distractions are removed. Pilgrimages are very powerful with the ones to Medjugorje, in my experience being the most powerful. Medjugorje is a small village in Croatia and one where the mother of Jesus has been appearing every day since 1981. I am one of over 70 million people who have been there and when I say 70 million people, I am referring to heads of state, bishops, powerful business men and wo-

When you take on fighting "evil," prayer needs to be a constant in your life.

men, etc. There have been thousands of miraculous cures in Medjugorje. The purpose of the cures is to get people's attention so that they will take seriously the messages that God is giving through Mary. You can Google this to read the messages and you can go there. For everyone who goes to Medjugorje, their spiritual life is deepened in a profound way and by everyone I am also referring to Jews, Muslims and both devout and lukewarm Christians.

If you have the ability to organize people and can show them how they can make an impact, they will work with you. If you want to be a great leader, it would be worthwhile to study how Martin Luther King Jr. took on racism. Not only was he an effective organizer, he brilliantly manipulated the perception of people in a way that gained nationwide support for his cause. The award winning movie "Come Walk in My Shoes," gives one a powerful sense as to how he accomplished this. Martin Luther King Jr. greatly admired Gandhi. *(14.1)* He enrolled his congregation in taking on a non-violent approach to racism. He understood the stereotype of "dumb and poor blacks" so he put out there front and center, well dressed, highly educated, well spoken, black college kids to simply go to "white only" soda fountains, and ask for a soda.

When the college kids were harassed, they continued to be respectful and polite. What happened is that some of the people in the soda fountain and coffee shops, who were white and racists themselves, told the bullies to leave the kids alone. If those kids had gotten angry, there would have been far less sympathy from the other customers. They may have gotten angry back, as technically the college kids were breaking the law by being in a "whites only" diner. Martin Luther King Jr. understood the power of perception and trained those college kids to be polite no matter what names they were called.

His slogan was "Freedom Now" and he convinced people that freedom was possible. People would not have bothered to fight with him if they did not think they could make a difference in achieving that goal. Ultimately, it was the picture in the newspaper of well-dressed families on a peaceful march being hosed down by police, which got the attention of the nation and was the start of profound change.

People will always respond based on their perception of the facts, not the facts themselves. The facts may have been that black people were being treated unfairly but if what people saw were roughnecks throwing bottles at the police, the incident would have ended very differently. Instead of protecting the black people from corruption and unfair treatment the National Guard would have been called down to Mississippi to put the "rioters" in jail. Martin Luther King Jr. was a brilliant organizer, a God inspired speaker and a master at motivating people to get out there and fight, even when the odds were against them. You will need to do the same, which is why Chapter Two was included in this book.

It is so tempting to vent, gossip and complain. That will only reinforce the perception that winning will be difficult and people do not want to participate if the project is going to be too difficult. Most people are willing to volunteer two to ten hours a month. If you can break down what you need in those increments, you will find a lot of people who want to work with you if you can convince them that their time spent will make a difference. You just need to create realistic expectations. Two to ten hours a month over a year can completely alter the life of another person. It won't happen in three meetings with a kid who needs your help.

Human Trafficking can be a brutal project to take on. The stories of the victims will tear your heart apart. Workers will share with you about a condition called "compassion exhaustion" where you start to become numb to the suffering of others. Personally, I limit how much I read about the suffering of the victims because at some point I become paralyzed with grief or so righteously indignant, I am liable to go off "half-cocked" in my pursuit of protecting potential victims, rather than using a strategic plan.

It is important to focus on joy, on the miracles that are happening, lest we burn out. For those who feel they need help developing a sense of joy, Kay Warren has a great study plan in her book "Choose Joy, Because Happiness Isn't Enough." I recently read a book that woke me up to how I have suppressed my joy because of my guilt about being too happy, given how much suffering there is in the world. In his book,

"Between Heaven and Earth, Why Joy, Humor and Laughter are at the Heart of the Spiritual Life," James Martin, who is a Jesuit priest, suggests that we have inherited a notion as Christians of a somber and serious Christ. As a result, in an effort to imitate Him, we have put a lid on our joy. He makes the case that Jesus was fun to be around and points out that in His time many parables of Jesus would have left people laughing.

One of the examples he used that Christians are familiar with is the parable that refers to noticing the speck in your neighbor's eye instead of the log in your own eye. James claims that the parable made its point in a way that would have gotten a laugh. To further illustrate the man of joy that Jesus was, James Martin cites the following biblical quote..."John came neither eating or drinking....the Son of Man came eating and drinking and they say "Look, a glutton and a drunkard." Apparently Jesus was having a good time! We should too, as it will regenerate us.

I start my day with "Your Best Life Begins Each Morning" by Joel Osteen and I go to mass. If I am feeling stressed I play rock and roll Christian praise music and sing at the top of my lungs. It always puts me in a good mood. Some "advocate" types are too intense for many people. You need to be enjoyable to be around if you are going to lead. I make it a point to eat well, exercise and play. When I am tired, I get discouraged. Those of us who are leaders are often good at giving but are sometimes not very receptive to receiving. We need to be responsible for letting others contribute to us, so we don't get burned out. Personally, what keeps me motivated is reading the Covenant House newsletter every month. Reading about kids who have endured torture and abuse and are still able to turn their life around inspires me to get to work. It is not the tragedy that motivates me. It is knowing that my efforts may provide another human being with the resources they need for a future worth having that moves me into action.

In addressing any social issue, we always want to look for root causes if we are going to end the problem. Clearly poverty is a root cause of Human Trafficking with illiteracy and lack of economic opportunity being one of the root causes of poverty. Porn addiction contributes to

Human Trafficking and divorce. Runaways are the most likely victims of Human Trafficking. Children run away because of abuse. One of the contributing factors to child abuse is drug addiction. So anything that we can do to reduce poverty, drug addiction and child abuse is addressing root causes for Trafficking.

Divorce is a root cause for many women and their children becoming homeless, making them vulnerable to becoming trafficked. A large percent of children who have been in the foster care system wind up in prison or worse, so it would seem that anything you do to support family stability, like establishing the "Safe Families" program at your place of worship, addresses the root cause of many social problems. Most places of worship have programs to support marriage and anything you do to support or participate in those programs is also doing your part to support family stability. Creating economic opportunities and supporting strong families addresses almost every social problem from drug addiction to poverty. I bring this up because sometimes people feel pressure to give up what they are called to do in other areas because "Human Trafficking" is a "hot" topic. We don't want to minimize all the good work that is being done on other issues.

For those of you who are fighting for peace, war creates orphans and destroys economies, which create an environment where Trafficking flourishes. By fighting for peace, you are doing your part to save children from becoming exploited by those who take advantage of the weakest among us. There are many efforts like this that make an impact in fighting Trafficking.

According to Oxfam, climate change is the single biggest factor to winning the battle against global hunger. Oxfam is to be commended for their "Behind the Brand" petitions. So far they have succeeded in convincing both Kellogg and General Mills to cut greenhouse gas emissions in their manufacturing and production processes as well as in their agricultural supply chains. Hunger in the Third World and Climate Change are making families more vulnerable to becoming Trafficking victims. If these two issues are on your heart, then go to the Oxfam site and help them by signing their petitions under "Take Action. In the

U.S., go to Oxfam America. This organization gets to the heart of the matter which is that "Hunger isn't about too many people and too little food. It's about power." www.oxfam.org

The ten hottest years on record have occurred since 1998. (14.2) The fact is that Climate Change is going to exacerbate every social problem on the planet, including but not limited to Human Trafficking. We don't even know the impact on our food supply of increased CO2 emissions and the thousands of plumes of methane gas that is being released as the Artic melts. Currently plant life is absorbing half of all CO2 on the planet. However, the strip mining that is destroying forests and the devastation of the Amazon jungle is quickly reducing the amount of plant life, which is accelerating Global Warming. According to the book "Ten Billion" by Stephen Emmott, all our "green energy" solutions are going to take too long to implement, to make a difference. According to Emmott, we need to immediately start consuming a lot less of anything that consumes a lot of water and fossil fuel before it is too late. The EPA is telling us that government needs to immediately implement the "Clean Power Plan" to reduce carbon emissions and we as citizens need to act when there is political push-back from those companies who are profiting from fossil fuels. Since the kinds of actions it will take to consume less will not be popular, many governments are not pushing hard enough to make that happen. So it is up to us to speak up and act.

While recycling and unplugging your phone chargers when not in use will help, we need to think much, much bigger. All companies need to incorporate a "green" policy as part of their corporate mission. In addition to reducing greenhouse emissions as part of their manufacturing process, how about every company employing "flex" work hours so people work four days a week instead of five or spend more time working from home. That alone would dramatically reduce fuel consumption from cars. We need a grass roots demand that will require corporations and government to employ as many innovative solutions as possible to reduce greenhouse gases before our planet becomes inhabitable. If you are looking to get involved and want to be part of a faith initiative, simply google "Christians, Global Warming" or "Jews, Global Warming" etc. If your friends are passionate about the environment, you could join forces and create an event that expresses both your passions. Your event could educate people on how to protect the environment, save energy and reduce Global Warming and include a "Fair Trade" table at that event. You could call the event "Justice for the Planet."

In addition to encouraging people to reduce their use of fossil fuels, with global warming we know water will be an issue as well as available land to grow food. People are motivated by solutions, so include a 3 ft. by 5 ft. display of a "vertical aquaponic vegetable garden" that grows fish and produces 200 heads of lettuce a year, using 2% of the water of traditional farming. (www.instructables.com/id/Build-a-vertical-aquaponic-veggie-fish-farm-for-/) At your Fair Trade table, you could sell reusable metal water bottles and re-usable bags that save the environment with slogans on the bags and bottles that promote Fair Trade. Doing something like this allows you to "piggyback" on the efforts of others to promote the cause you are passionate about and allows you to support a group that is raising awareness regarding an issue like Global Warming, which also impacts your cause. Give yourself permission to be creative. Follow your heart and always have fun!

At the Restorative Justice symposium in 2012, Matthew Cate who at that time was Secretary of the California Department of Corrections and Rehabilitation, was a keynote speaker. He began his talk by reviewing current statistics. Then at one point he stopped, paused for a minute then launched into an impassioned speech. Essentially what he said was ...."If you want to help me reduce recidivism (the return rate) in California prisons, I need for you to go back to your churches and get a bus. Then take that bus up to my prison and spend some time teaching someone to read. Your willingness to spend time with someone to provide what they need gives that person a sense of value. Instilling in someone a sense of their own value, is the most effective thing I have seen that keeps people from returning to prison." *(14.3)*

That statement is the essence of what true ministry is. By giving someone a sense of their own value they are empowered to make better choices. We can do that as a foster parent, a mentor or someone who works with the poor or with someone in prison. Actually, it is in serving others that we learn the essence of our own true value.

We can't afford to allow discouragement to make us quit. These kids are depending on us. They have no one else. One former victim shared about running away from her pimp and hiding behind a trash can. Then she asked herself, where could she go? When she realized that she had no place to go, that no one cared, she went back to her pimp knowing the beatings that would await her because she felt that was her only option. Trafficking victims need to know that the world does care about what happens to them. They need hope and for us to be there for them.

When the "The Center for Missing and Exploited Children" began in 1984 their success rate for finding kids was 67%. It is now 97%. Through our churches, synagogues, temples, mosques, parent groups and community organizations, we have the ability to achieve a similar success rate with regard to preventing kids from becoming trafficked and rescuing those who have. We just need to start with one thing and trust God to lead us to what we need to do next and continue to grow our efforts.

We have the resources to take care of every social problem on the planet, we just need to figure out what needs to be done, organize ourselves to do it and get out there and fight. If you would like to help us raise awareness as to what people can do, please share the book and post a review at Amazon. If you "like" our Facebook page you will get updates on what government and organizations are doing to fight Human Trafficking. Just search for "How You Can Fight Human Trafficking." It is clear that God has heard the cries of his children and is calling the entire world to take on the cause of justice with every individual discovering and making their own unique contribution. It is my prayer that this book will support you in doing that.

*References: (14.1) Placido P. D'Souza, January 20, 2013, Commemorating Martin Luther King Jr. / Gandhi's influence on King. San Francisco Gate online
(14.2) "Ten Billion," by Stephan Emmott
(14.3) Matthew Cate, Keynote Speaker. Symposium on "Crime, Punishment and the Common Good in California." 8/3/2012, Marymount College, Los Angeles*

Supplement One-How to Bring A Mini Human Trafficking Conference to a Place of Worship

It is a lot of work to put together a conference and if the people in your community are not already convinced that Human Trafficking is a problem, then they won't be interested enough to come to a conference. So I prayed about this and the Holy Spirit gave me the idea of how to bring a "mini" conference to a church to raise awareness and create ministries at churches to fight Trafficking. The following approach is working brilliantly as it makes it possible to raise awareness among thousands of people in one day and facilitate them in getting involved in the fight.

You are welcome to duplicate this approach and can use the talk on the next page as a model and incorporate examples that are relevant to the area you are in. Since I speak in Southern California, I mention the number of runaways that come to SoCal, as that is a relevant issue for this part of the country. You will need to research where Trafficking is happening in your community so you can bring this crime "home" to the people you speak to, as less people will act if they think human trafficking is happening somewhere other than where they live. Invite groups that are working in your community for issues like gang activity if that applies. Always invite foster care and mentoring to have a table outside to recruit volunteers. A local rehabilitation group is also a good one to invite as they make this issue "real" for people.

I do a 5 minute talk at the end of each service. Outside are tables from different agencies so people can immediately go outside and get their questions answered and sign up to go to an orientation for Adoption/Foster care, or mentoring or for a street outreach ministry like Covenant House or Stand Up for Kids. I host a table for advocacy and have recent newspaper articles, flyers from Rescue and Restore, Fair Trade and one explaining what Human Trafficking is, etc.

Many people have thought of becoming a foster parent or want to go out and find kids on the street, but they don't know where to start. If I all I did was talk and then let them go home to figure out how to find out more information on becoming a foster parent etc., it is not very likely that much would happen. For instance if one Google's "foster parenting," they get thousands of responses. It is too overwhelming so they leave it for another day and nothing happens. The talk creates a sense of urgency to help kids and they have an immediate opportunity to fulfill on their desire to do that at the tables outside.

Every time I do this talk, we recruit a handful of prospective foster/adoptive parents to go to an orientation, 25 to 40 people who commit to go to a meeting to find out what is involved in mentoring and dozens who sign up to find out more about volunteering for a street outreach organization. Before people will even go to an orientation, they need general questions answered so we do that.

I always set up a ministry whenever I speak by announcing the first meeting when I do the talk and use the ideas in this book at the follow up meeting to empower both individuals and the group to take action. The pastors love this approach because they feel that the church is doing their part to protect kids and reduce demand. All they need to do is schedule the time I can speak and provide a room for the follow up meeting. I often meet with the youth pastor beforehand who will share stories of how teens are being solicited, which I share with people when I do the follow up talk. At the first meeting, usually @25 to 80 people show up, depending on how many services I spoke at. This meeting is for anyone who wants to find out what they can do. Now that you have read this book, you can lead that meeting. Just bring the "Handout" that is at our site www.throughGodsgrace.com on the Human Trafficking tab. and email us ucanfightht@throughgodsgrace.com to get our powerpoint.

The first meeting is for parents so they can get information on how to protect their children and for anyone who may be curious as to what can be done. The second meeting is for people who want to be part of a ministry at the church, temple, synagogue, mosque, etc. and you should have that meeting scheduled before you speak at the first meeting so you can announce it. You can use Chapter Ten for ideas on how to run the second meeting.

At the first meeting, if you can't be the one who will be leading the second meeting, then ask who wants to be the facilitator for the second meeting. All that person has to do is to make sure there is a meeting once a month and make sure that some activity gets planned by the third meeting. I give "homework" at the first meeting to read the handout and go to the websites and suggest that people do their own research regarding what is on their heart and be ready to share ideas for how they want to participate by the next meeting. For the leader, I give them a copy of this book and suggest that for those who are passionate about this issue, they should purchase the book.

I have done this talk many times and have revised it every time I got feedback or a complaint. I originally said "kids were forced into the sex trade," instead of the phrase "kids become victims of Human Trafficking." Parents did not like me using the word "sex," probably because their children might have asked them what I was talking about as even little kids know that word means something significant. I used to say that "the Traffickers tortured and terrorized their victims and the kids were dead in 3 to 7 years." Parents objected because it scared their children. So I changed it to "due to how brutal the life is, their life expectancy is 3 to 7 years. " That way, the talk goes over the head of a little kid and you want to do it that way if you are speaking after a service with families in the room. Just letting you know, because you don't want complaints, otherwise the pastor may not support what you are trying to accomplish. Here is the talk.....

My name is ....and my purpose here this morning is to share with you what you can do to fight Human Trafficking. The California Attorney General tells us that a Trafficker can make well over half a million dollars a year making this crime the fastest growing criminal enterprise in this country and one where law enforcement needs our help. According to the Center for Missing and Exploited Children, over 100,000 kids under the age of 18 are victimized by Human Trafficking in the U.S. Contrary to popular belief, @70% of these kids will be U.S Citizens.

Every year, over 300,000 teenage runaways will come to Southern California and who is waiting for them are the Human Traffickers. In Southern California, 40% of the kids who age out of the foster care system will become homeless. Within 48 hours of a kid hitting the streets, 1 out 3 will be approached by a Human Trafficker. Once they are picked up, due to how brutal the life is their life expectancy will be 3 to 7 years. Only 1% will ever be rescued.

These kids need our help and protection and there are 2 main actions we can take to accomplish that. First we will have a meeting on (date and time) here at (name of Faith Community.) We will educate you on what you personally can do to stop this cruel exploitation of children. Half the meeting will be information for parents on how to protect their own children. 100% of children online will be approached by someone who wants to exploit them. Given how clever these criminals are at tricking kids, it is important that every parent be at the meeting.

The second action is to intervene in the lives of the most likely victim, who are kids from the foster care system and homeless teens before the Traffickers pick them up. Their only hope for a future is to connect with an adult who cares about them. You can be that person as a foster or adoptive parent or a mentor to a kid in the foster care system or by volunteering for a street outreach organization. There is a real need for good foster and adoptive parents and if you have ever considered being a foster parent or know someone who has thought about foster parenting, or adoption (organization) is here in the courtyard to answer any questions you may have.

The Traffickers are targeting girls and boys in group homes and their best defense against being lured away by the Traffickers is to have a mentor and you can get more information regarding mentoring at the table for "Big brothers and Big Sisters." (You can substitute another mentoring organization like CASA here.)

Covenant House (or local street outreach organization) goes out to the streets to try and find these kids before the Traffickers do. They help the kids obtain an apartment, their GED, a job, hope for a better future and they have information at their table regarding their volunteer opportunities.

(If you are in a gang community, this is where you could invite a group to come who rehabilitates gang members and say something like "Given that gangs are heavily involved in Trafficking in our community, (name of organization) is here today to share with you the work they are doing to reform gang members. And/or if you are in an immigrant community you could invite someone from a group that works with immigrants and say "Given that the Traffickers prey on immigrants, (name of organization) is here today to share with you their volunteer opportunities so you can work with them to protect immigrant families.)

If I have a letter to the president for people to sign to ask him to establish "opt in" in the U.S., I mention that here and invite people to come to my table to sign it. (Letter sample on the next page) Then I say "The volunteers from the different organizations have generously given of their time today. Please do take a few minutes to stop by their tables to get more information regarding what you can do to protect kids and do come to the meeting on (date and time.) We need to act before it is too late!"

SAMPLE LETTER FOR "OPT IN"

Dear President Obama,

We urge you to follow the lead of Prime Ministry Cameron of England and establish a business regulation in the U.S. that requires all internet providers to block all porn at the provider's site unless one "Opts In." This will protect our children from accessing porn on their cell phones as the individual who pays for the service is the one who has to "Opt In." It will impact the porn pandemic and reduce the demand for sex trafficking, the fastest growing crime in the U.S. Given how violent porn has become, this action will also impact violence against women, a pandemic in the U.S. Given that 56% of divorces cite internet pornography as a contributing factor in the breakup of their marriage, this action will contribute to stronger families. As you well know, the breakup of the family contributes to many social problems.

In addition, we ask that your administration take on eliminating extremely violent and "Barely Legal" porn. In addition, please require that all internet providers block child porn like Google and Microsoft has done. Given that the U.S. produces half of all child porn in the world, we need to be more aggressive at prosecuting offenders.

Please act today!

Supplement Two-Pumpkin Pie Spice, Fair Trade Chai Tea

(Excerpt from the book "15 Minute Healthy Organic Meals for Less Than $10 a Day")

People ask me all the time how I have the energy to work a full time job, raise children and speak to thousands every year on fighting Human Trafficking. The answer is I take good care of myself and I do it in very little time. I have spent so much time sharing how I organize everything on a budget to eat nutritious, organic, low sugar/acid meals that as I mentioned in Chapter Four, I decided to write an e-book that promotes using Fair Trade products and sells for $5.99 outlining quick meals you can make. The book is entitled "15 Minute Healthy Organic Meals for Less Than $10 a Day." The fully illustrated print book sells for $19.95 and if you purchase the print book, the e-book is free.

While containing many recipes, the book will not be a cookbook per se. It will be a plan for how to make eating and living really healthy work with a busy lifestyle for very little money. It will include where one can buy Fair Trade Products, twenty four examples of acid/alkaline balanced hearty meals, how to bake gluten free, how in three minutes you can make enough cold brew coffee to last you two weeks, thereby reducing the acid in your coffee by 67% etc.

Disease, arthritis, etc. loves acid conditions and our diet is almost all acidic foods. Too many poor mothers are feeding their children "top ramen" when they could be feeding them brown rice for 50 cents a pound, cooked. Healthy organic snack bars are expensive, @$3.50 for 1.5 ounces or @$32 a pound, but you can make them for @$6 a pound. Organic Fair Trade chocolate bars cost @$1 an ounce. I will show you how to make fudge for 40 cents an ounce. If you are a soda drinker, the book will show you how to make non-diary kefir pro-biotic soda and Kombucha, which tastes delicious, has 15% of the sugar of soda and boosts your immune system for 50 cents a glass.

The Food and Agricultural Organization of the United Nations (FAO) has determined that a significant percent of the world's diseases would be eliminated if people substituted quinoa for white rice. Quinoa is the only grain that is a complete protein and it has significant nutritional and anti-inflammatory properties. So why am I bringing this up in a book on Human Trafficking? The answer is, because one of the overall themes of the book is to show people that we have the resources to have the world work for everyone. Simply changing from white rice to quinoa could eliminate a lot of misery in the world caused by disease and disease makes the poor even poorer. If your body hurts, then you might want to consider eliminating all inflammatory and acidic foods from your diet like gluten, sugar, dairy, coffee and meat.

What about behavior? We have so many teens diagnosed with "bipolar" disorder and "defiant" disorder, sometimes acting out in violent ways. Yes, they have issues and hormone imbalances, but if I lived on Cheetos and Coke, I would cry easily, be very irritable and exhausted all the time. Many families get a better outcome from counseling by including a healthy diet as part of their program. By considering food as one of the root causes of many social problems like disease, depression, etc., we would be motivated to take steps to correct our diet.

In addition to detoxifying your body and providing anti-oxidants with Chai Tea, (recipe on the next page) every day should start with a high protein breakfast because it boosts your metabolism which helps you feel alert and energetic. The best way to accomplish this without the bulk of a heavy breakfast, which will make you feel sluggish is with a protein drink. You can purchase high quality organic protein powder at a reasonable price at www.truenutrition.com. You can use this code "jdk127" for a 10% discount. The reason why the prices are so reasonable is because you aren't paying for packaging and advertising.

You can include the "Super Greens" powder, @10% so that you get your greens every make your drink more alkaline. The Grass Fed whey insures you get vitamin K2. Add flax seeds for fiber and Chia Seeds for fiber to keep you "regular" every day, so that you are eliminating toxins, otherwise you may be sluggish and tired. Add 1/8 teaspoon stevia, a little fresh fruit and half a banana and you will be in heaven while consuming over 20 grams of protein for @$3 a drink. To lose weight, make your drink with water. To gain weight, add a banana and coconut oil.

Pumpkin Pie Spice Chai Tea

Many families in India have their favorite Chai Tea recipe that has been handed down for generations. You are about to continue this tradition by determining what recipe works best for you. This works best if you make enough for a week and then put in a mason jar or the like, so all you have to do is take a minute to heat it up in the morning. This recipe makes 6 cups of tea. When you add the milk, the total is 8 to 9 cups of tea. The health benefits of each ingredient are numerous. If you look each one up, you will never go a day without drinking chai again given what it does for your body. We have put in parenthesis the main benefits. Slave labor is used in the tea, sugar and spice industry, so make sure you are using "Fair Trade" tea, sugar and spices.

Ingredients

6 Fair Trade cardamom pods. (antioxidant) Open them up, toss the pods and crush the seeds.
1 inch, fresh organic ginger. (anti-inflammatory)
Pinch of black or Fair Trade cayenne pepper. (purifies the blood)
1 tsp Fair Trade cinnamon. (manages blood sugar)
3 shakes of Fair Trade nutmeg. (reverses aging)
4 Fair Trade cloves that have been broken up. (antibacterial)
4 tsp organic, Fair Trade tea.
3 cups water.
¼ tsp stevia and 2 TB spoons organic, Fair Trade sugar.

Add spices, bring water to a boil. Turn heat off and add tea and sweetener. Let steep for 20 minutes. Pour tea through a strainer into a mason jar or other vessel that has a lid. It can be hot, but not so hot that it breaks your jar. Fill the pot back up with 1.5 cups water and put through the strainer again. Then fill up the pot again with another 1.5 cups water and pour into your container so you get all the tea from the leaves out.

Now the fun begins! Pour a little into a cup, add the amount of milk or cream you usually drink with your tea and taste it. If you want more cinnamon, add it. If tea is too weak, then steep some more tea. If too strong, add water. If you like the taste of cardamom, then use 8 pods next time. If you want it spicier, add more pepper and ginger. However, if you make it too spicy it might make you feel a little nauseous if you drink spicy tea on an empty stomach. If you want your tea to taste like "Starbucks" then you need to use cream and @2-4 TB of sugar per cup, depending on the size of your cup. Look up Chai Tea recipes and experiment so that one time, you try "allspice" instead of cardamom or try adding anise. Try cream, almond milk or organic soy milk. Add more sweetener if you prefer, but don't use any other artificial sweetener except Stevia. Stevia has a slightly bitter aftertaste, but if you combine it with sugar, you can't taste it. Perfect your "family recipe!" The tea will keep for a week. Just heat it up in the morning and add your milk. Don't store the milk in your jar as the stored milk can sour your tea. Best not to store in a plastic container or your tea will start to taste like plastic.

If you are a major coffee drinker, then make "dirty" chai. If you add coffee to the mason jar, then your tea will become acid. So what I recommend you do is put a 3/4 cup of tea in your pot in the morning and add 1 teaspoon of coffee with ¼ cup water and heat it up. Add the milk before taking the tea off the stove and strain the coffee out. "Dirty Chai" is delicious. After drinking it for a few days, regular coffee will seem so bland. "Dirty Chai" is less acidic then regular coffee. If you are not using organic coffee, you are pouring toxins into your body as non-organic coffee is one of the most sprayed agricultural products in the world.

Enjoy Your Tea!

Acknowledgements

I have met hundreds of people who I greatly admire who are my heroes and heroines in the campaign to end Human Trafficking. Carissa Phelps, Rachel Thomas, Shyima Hall and Harmony Dust are all great examples of former victims who are using their experience to step out and make a difference. Pastor Paula Daniels and Sandra Morgan are two examples of people who saw a need and stepped out and made something happen, with very little or no experience. That takes courage.

Then there are exceptional leaders in the fight against the exploitation of children who deserve special mention. They are David Batstone and Kevin Bales, both authors of outstanding books on what it will take to end slavery worldwide. Ernie Allen, cofounder of "The Center for Missing and Exploited Children," Donna Rice Hughes of Enough.org and Patrick Trueman, founder of Porn Harms; who are all leading the fight against pornography are to be commended for responding to what God called them to do. The community leaders, Homeland Security, the police, social workers, probation workers, teachers and faith leaders that I talked to are all the hardest working people I know in the fight to protect people from this cruel crime and deserve our prayers and support as their job is not easy. I especially want to thank all the people who I have worked with to set up a ministry at their church who continue to inspire and encourage me. For that I am eternally grateful.

About the Author

Like many of you, after learning of the suffering of so many children who are victims of Human Trafficking, Susan Patterson, Director of Through God's Grace Ministry, prayed and asked God what she should do. She thought of the victims all the time, tossing and turning at night, waking up to pray for them, putting several plans together. God gave her no peace until she got to work. What God showed her is that she should use her speaking, consulting and motivational skills as well as her experience in church ministry to raise awareness and start a movement to engage Faith Communities to act. At first she went out and raised awareness among thousands, at local churches, of the fact that Human Trafficking was happening right in their own neighborhoods. When people came up to her table after the talk to ask questions, the most common question was "What can I as a nurse, homemaker, teen, attorney, teacher, businessman, etc. do to fight trafficking?"

So Susan went out and spent countless hours attending numerous conferences and spoke to close to a hundred people made up of community and church leaders, conference speakers, Homeland Security, the police, DA's, social workers, NGO's, victims and people just like you with the question "What can we do to fight Human Trafficking?" She began to use the information she had learned in her talks and people could not get the information down fast enough. The most common response to her talks was "I had heard about Human Trafficking but did not know what I could personally do about it." Now I know and I really appreciate the opportunity to have found that out." This book is the result of all those interviews and Susan's experience in working with dozens of faith communities to fight Human Trafficking. It is designed to empower anyone, no matter what their age or station in life, to take on the fight against the cruel exploitation of children and adults.